MAKING MORE WOODEN MECHANICAL MODELS

MAKING MORE
WOODEN
MECHANICAL
MODELS

ALAN AND GILL BRIDGEWATER

POPULAR WOODWORKING BOOKS
CINCINNATI, OHIO
www.popularwoodworking.com

Read This Important Safety Notice

To prevent accidents, keep safety in mind while you work. Use the safety guards installed on power equipment; they are for your protection. When working on power equipment, keep fingers away from saw blades, wear safety goggles to prevent injuries from flying wood chips and sawdust, wear headphones to protect your hearing, and consider installing a dust vacuum to reduce the amount of airborne sawdust in your woodshop. Don't wear loose clothing, such as neckties or shirts with loose sleeves, or jewelry, such as rings, necklaces or bracelets, when working on power equipment. Tie back long hair to prevent it from getting caught in your equipment. People who are sensitive to certain chemicals should check the chemical content of any product before using it. The author and editors who compiled this book have tried to make the contents as accurate and correct as possible. Plans, illustrations, photographs and text have been carefully checked. All instructions, plans and projects should be carefully read, studied and understood before beginning construction. Due to the variability of local conditions, construction materials, skill levels, etc., neither the author nor Popular Woodworking Books assumes any responsibility for any accidents, injuries, damages or other losses incurred resulting from the material presented in this book.

Making More Wooden Mechanical Models. Copyright © 2000 by Alan and Gill Bridgewater. Manufactured in China. All rights reserved. No part of this book may be reproduced in any form or by any electronic or mechanical means including information storage and retrieval systems without permission in writing from the publisher, except by a reviewer, who may quote brief passages in a review. Published by Popular Woodworking Books, an imprint of F&W Publications, Inc., 1507 Dana Avenue, Cincinnati, Ohio, 45207. First edition.

Other fine Popular Woodworking Books are available from your local bookstore or direct from the publisher.

Visit our Web site at www.popularwoodworking.com for information on more resources for woodworkers.

04   03   02   01   00   5   4   3   2   1

Library of Congress Cataloging-in-Publication Data

Bridgewater, Alan.
    Making more wooden mechanical models / by Alan and Gill Bridgewater. – 1st ed.
       p. cm.
    Includes index.
    ISBN 1-55870-508-2 (alk. paper)
    1. Woodwork Amateurs' manuals. 2. Machinery--Models Amateurs' manuals. 3. Models and modelmaking Amateurs' manuals. I. Title.
TT185.B735 1999
621.8'022'8—dc21   99-21732
                                            CIP

Edited by Michael Berger, Mark Thompson
Designed by Wendy Dunning
Production coordinated by Erin Boggs
Cover photography by Greg Grosse

METRIC CONVERSION CHART		
TO CONVERT	**TO**	**MULTIPLY BY**
Inches	Centimeters	2.54
Centimeters	Inches	0.4
Feet	Centimeters	30.5
Centimeters	Feet	0.03
Yards	Meters	0.9
Meters	Yards	1.1
Sq. Inches	Sq. Centimeters	6.45
Sq. Centimeters	Sq. Inches	0.16
Sq. Feet	Sq. Meters	0.09
Sq. Meters	Sq. Feet	10.8
Sq. Yards	Sq. Meters	0.8
Sq. Meters	Sq. Yards	1.2
Pounds	Kilograms	0.45
Kilograms	Pounds	2.2
Ounces	Grams	28.4
Grams	Ounces	0.04

DEDICATION

We would like to dedicate this book to the world wide web of woodworkers—all the hundreds of thousands of men and women all over the world—who are happily beavering away in their workshops busily making items in wood. I can see them now, in little sheds in city yards, in sheds in forest glades, in sheds in Canada, and England, and Ireland, in Australia—in sheds all over the world. Young folk just starting out, middle aged men and women who are seeking respite from their stress-filled working lives, old folk who are enjoying retirement, hundreds of thousands of people—young and old, rich and poor—all working in their sheds making items in wood.

ACKNOWLEDGMENTS

We would like to thank all the manufacturers who have supplied us with the best of the best—especially:

Jim Brewer, Research and Marketing Manager, Freud
P.O. Box 7187, 218 Feld Ave.
High Point, NC 27264 USA
(Forstner drill bits)

John P. Jodkin, Vice President, Delta International
Machine Corp.
246 Alpha Drive
Pittsburgh, PA 15238-2985 USA
(Band saws)

Dawn Fretz, Marketing Assistant, De-Sta-Co
P.O. Box 2800
Troy, MI 48007 USA
(Clamps)

Most of all, we would like to thank Friedrich Wilhelm Emmerich—E.C. EMMERICH PLANES, Herderstrabe 7, Remscheid, Germany—for his beautiful wooden planes. They are special! If you are looking to set yourself up with the best of all modern planes, then these are the ones to go for.

Last but not least, we would like to thank Adam Blake for his dynamic enthusiasm—a real inspiration.

TABLE OF CONTENTS

Introduction...8

PROJECT 1
Steam Crank Slider Mechanism...................9

PROJECT 2
Differential Pulley Block...........................17

PROJECT 3
The Excentric Squirrel Fan......................26

Gallery...33

PROJECT 4
Six Valve Radial Engine..................................46

PROJECT 5
Wheel & Worm Gear Mechanism..............54

PROJECT 6
Film Advancing Mechanism........................62

PROJECT 7
The Universal Joint.......................................70

PROJECT 8
Camshaft Valve...78

PROJECT 9
Water Lift Pump...86

PROJECT 10
Lever & Ratchet Mechanism.....................93

PROJECT 11
Screw Jack...101

PROJECT 12
The Bicycle Chain Machine.....................110

PROJECT 13
The Wonderful Wilmhurst Machine.......118

Index...126

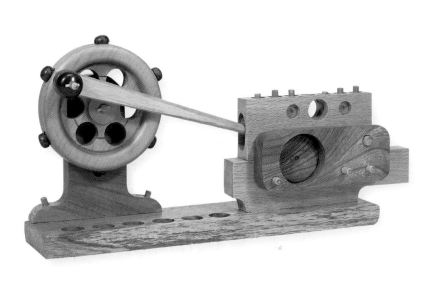

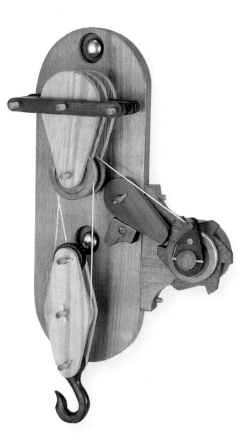

My grandpa used to tell my mother that I was one of those complicated sticky-fingered little boys who needed watching! He always used to say that I was up to tricks and learning. As I remember, all this meant, in effect, was that I was borrowing tools without permission, usually missing at meal times, and generally difficult to track down. It wasn't that I was in any way naughty or up to no good, but rather that I was always "inventing." I made a cross bow that was more a lethal man trap than a weapon, an electric alarm clock that couldn't be touched unless you were wearing rubber gloves, a lever mechanism for the gate that very nearly skinned and quartered the neighbor's cat, and so the list goes on. So you see, it wasn't that I was a horrible little boy bent on mischief, but only that I loved mechanisms and enjoyed working with tools and wood.

I was never so happy as when I was tucked away in the back shed hacking away with knife and saw on one or other of my labour saving inventions.

And of course, now that I am a man and fully grown, one of my chief pleasures is being out in my shed workshop dreaming up new mechanisms. But I'm not alone! The miraculous thing, the thing that makes our marriage so successful, is that my wife Gill is a soul mate, a true kindred spirit. We both get pleasure working with wood. Picture us if you will...out in our workshop, the radio humming away, our two dogs fast asleep in a couple of ancient armchairs, mugs of tea, both of us up to our armpits in a glorious miasma of tools, shavings, beeswax, wood and working drawings. Our shed workshop is a haven! And now that our two sons are out of the nest, it doesn't matter too much if we spend most of the night working. If we are tired but still willing, we simply settle down in the armchairs with a knife and

whatever part needs sorting, and drift and dream away the hours. The incredible thing is that at the end of it all—after hour upon hour spent sawing, planing, gouging, turning, whittling and waxing—we get to make the most amazingly intricate machines and mechanisms.

As I said in our first book on machines—*Making Wooden Mechanical Models*—our ambitions involve sharing with you the pleasures of creating small machines and mechanical prototypes from wood. We want you to share in the fun. The projects are small, so you don't need a vast workshop full of tools or a fortune in wood, all you need is enthusiasm.

With each of the thirteen projects, we take you through all the wonderfully satisfying procedures of choosing the wood, setting out the designs, sawing, planing, drilling and all the rest. We give you working drawings and template designs to explain how, why and what-with. There are drawings showing details, and there are photographs to explain the various step-by-step stages. We have done our best to describe all the procedures that go into making our working wooden wonders.

Each project draws inspiration from a specific mechanism. There are thirteen projects in all—all exciting, all dynamic, all beautiful and all made from wood.

Making More Wooden Mechanical Models is about the quiet personal pleasures of using your head, heart and hands to create uniquely beautiful machines in wood.

What else to say except that we now picture in our minds a world wide web of woodworkers, all beavering away in their workshops—hundreds of thousands of men and women all in their little sheds—warm and toasty, and engrossed in making our machines. A wonderful vision isn't it! A world of people all happily communing with wood.

Steam Crank Slider Mechanism

PROJECT BACKGROUND

The steam crank slider mechanism is one of those joyous archetypal machines that sets me to thinking about steam trains and heavy industry. I'm sure you know what I mean, the good old bad days, a time before this, before plastics and computers, when just about everything to do with industry and plant was massively built in cast iron—lots of steam, grease, oil and noise!

This is a great machine to watch in action. When the handle is turned—either way—the crank moves backwards and forwards, and the piston is set to moving on its guide block.

PROJECT OVERVIEW

Have a look at the project picture above, the working drawing (Figure 1-2A) and the template design (Figure 1-2B), and see how the stanchion and the guide block are fitted to the base board so that the piston block is nicely in line with the crank. See also how the crank rod is fixed inside the piston block, so as to allow for the movement of both components.

Although the design is pretty straightforward—not too many precise measurements—you do have to be mindful that the relationship between the length of the rod and the length of the piston guide slot is critical. That said, if you do have doubts as to how the various slots and pins work one to another, then it's always a good idea to sort out potential problems by making a paper, pin and cardboard prototype.

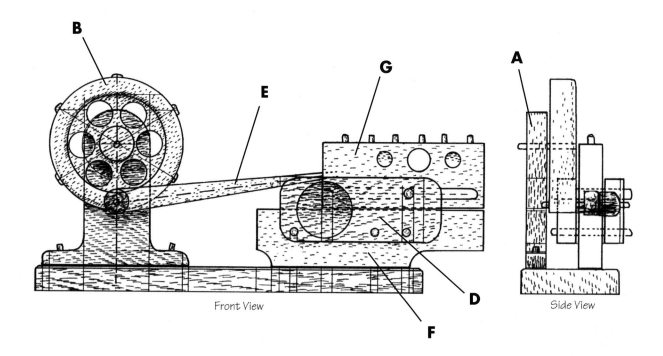

Front View

Side View

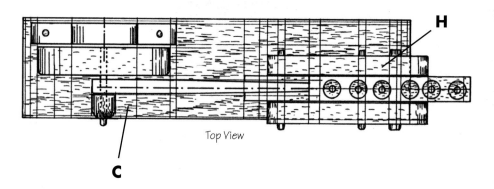

Top View

FIGURE 1-2A

A *Round-topped stanchion*
B *Flywheel*
C *Base board*
D *Guide plate*
E *Crank rod*
F *Guide block*
G *Piston block*
H *Guide plate*

PROJECT ONE: TEMPLATE DESIGN

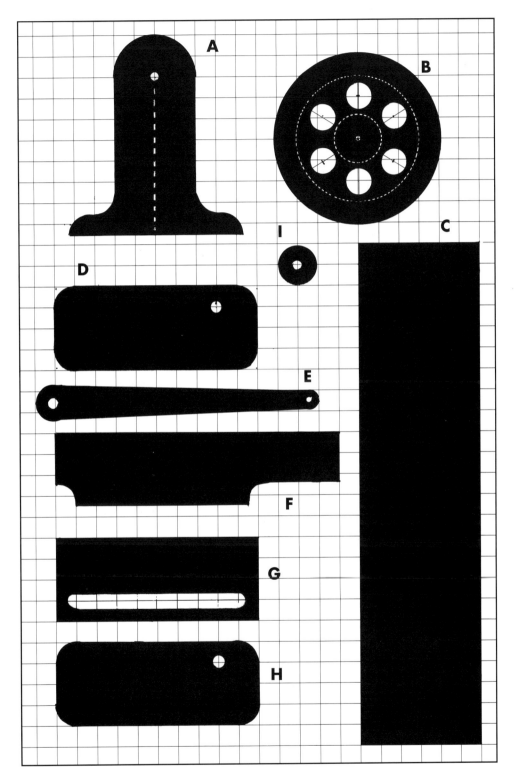

FIGURE 1-2B
The template design at a scale
of two grid squares to 1 inch.
A Round-topped stanchion
B Flywheel
C Base board
D Guide plate
E Crank rod
F Guide block
G Piston block
H Guide plate
I Spacer ring

NOTE
As with any wooden sculp-
ture, the dimensions indicated are starting points only.
Modify dimensions, spacers
and parts as necessary.

CUTTING LIST

Note: all measurements are in inches, and all sizes allow for a generous amount of cutting waste.

Part	Item	Dimensions T W L
A	Round-topped stanchion	¾ x 5 x 5½
B	Flywheel	1 x 5 x 5
C	Base board	1 x 4 x 13
D	Guide plate	¾ x 2½ x 5½
E	Crank rod	¾ x ¾ x 7
F	Guide block	1 x 2 x 8
G	Piston block	1 x 2½ x 5½
H	Guide plate	¾ x 2½ x 5½
I	Spacer ring	½ x 1 x 1

FIGURE 1-3
Use a shooting board and a smoothing plane to skim the edges to a crisp true finish. Reduce the friction by burnishing the cheeks of the plane with a white candle.

CHOOSING YOUR WOOD

This is one of those projects where just about anything goes—if you want to use pine throughout, or offcuts, then fine. That said, it is important that both the flywheel and the crank rod be made from easy-to-turn wood—something like lime, beech, or maple. It's no good trying to turn knotty oak!

We chose to use English brown oak for the base slab, stanchion and drive plates, beech for the guide block and the piston block, and lime for the wheel and the rod.

MAKING THE BASE SLAB

1 Take the piece of wood that you have chosen for the base slab, and use a rule and square to draw it out to size at 3"x12".

2 Cut the wood to size, and use a shooting board and smoothing plane to bring the slab to a good crisp finish (Figure 1-3).

3 Bevel to edges with a block plane. Pencil label the underside.

MAKING THE STANCHION

1 Use a pencil rule and compass to draw the stanchion to size on the workout paper—make changes to the profile if you have a mind to—and then use the same procedure to set the image out on your chosen piece of wood.

2 Fix the position of the pivot point and run it through with a bit to match the diameter of your dowel rod.

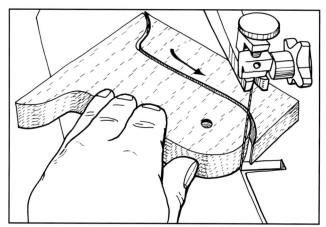

FIGURE 1-4
Work at a steady pace, all the while being ready to move the wood so that the blade is presented with the line of cut.

3 Use a scroll saw to fret out the form. Work at a nice easy pace, so that the line of cut is clean and fractionally to the waste side of the drawn line (Figure 1-4).

MAKING THE PISTON BLOCK AND SLIDING BLOCK

1 Cut the piston block to shape and size, and draw in the position of the guide rod slot.

2 While there are any number of ways of clearing the slot waste—you can use a drill and/or a coping saw and such like—I found that the easiest way, in this context, was to use a router bit in the pillar drill. Drill two holes right through the piece—one at each end of the slot—and then run the router bit backward and forward from hole to hole until you are through (Figure 1-5).

FIGURE 1-5
Run the workpiece backward and forward, while at the same time gently lowering the bit.

FIGURE 1-6
Fix the components on the base board with dry dowel. Note that the line of decorative drill sinkings was achieved with a Forstner bit.

3 Cut the piston guide block to size and shape—meaning the block on which the piston block sits—and dry fix it in place on the base slab with dowels (Figure 1-6). Fix the stanchion pillar in like manner.

4 Cut the two piston guide plates to size.

5 Having first turned the piston rod to shape and rubbed it down on opposite sides, drill a hole into the end of the piston block and use a loose-fit pin to fix the thin end of the rod in the hole.

6 Modify the shape of the piston hole until the rod is able to move up and down without hindrance (Figure 1-7).

7 Finally, sit the piston block on the guide block, set the two plates one on either side, and run a dowel through the plates so that the piston is contained (Figure 1-8).

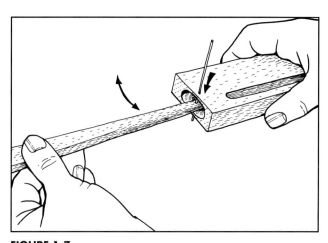

FIGURE 1-7
The pin needs to be a tight fit through the block and a loose easy fit through the end of the rod, so that the movement is free.

FIGURE 1-8
Adjust the fit of the plates and the length of the slot so that the extent of the run relates to the diameter of the flywheel.

FIGURE 1-9
Use the dividers to check off measurements and to step-off around the circumference. Note the rounded finish to the top face of the rim.

FIGURE 1-10
Use a pillar drill and a Forstner bit to run the holes through the thickness. Note how the turned line helps set the position of the center points.

MAKING THE FLYWHEEL

1 Take your piece of sawn wood at 1" thick and 5"x5" square, and check it over for problems—avoid anything that looks to be split or knotty. If you have doubts, then look for another piece.

2 Draw crossed diagonals across the 5"x5" slab to fix the position of the center point. Scribe a circle at 4½" diameter, and cut the blank disk out on the scroll saw.

3 Mount the disk on the lathe and turn it down to a finished diameter of 4¼" at about ⅞" thick.

4 Use a parting tool and the skew chisel to turn off the profiles that go to make up the design. Aim for a rim at about ½" wide, with the central boss being about 1" diameter, with the face of the boss being about ⅜" lower than the face of the rim (Figure 1-9).

5 Rub the disk to a smooth finish and remove from the lathe.

6 Having first used a compass to divide the circumference of the wheel into six equal segments, draw lines across the circle so as to create a six-spoke form, and then use the bit size of your choice to run six holes through the wheel (Figure 1-10).

FITTING THE CONNECTING ROD

1 When you are happy with the shape and finish of the wheel, and when you have drilled the holes for the central pivot and the handle, take the piston rod and continue sanding the two "flats" down to a smooth finish.

2 The best way forward is to rub the faces down on a lapping board—meaning a sheet of abrasive paper that has been mounted grit-face-up on a sheet of plywood (Figure 1-11). Continue until the distance across the resultant flats is equal to the diameter of the rod at the thin end.

3 Finally, have a trial fitting of the rod on the flywheel. If all is well, the wheel should be able to rotate with the flat face of the rod being in close but smooth contact—no twisting.

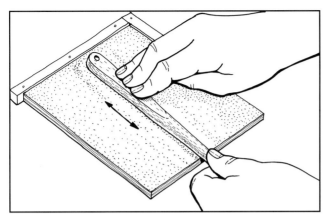

FIGURE 1-11
Rub the turning down at the broad end—until there are two distinct flats, with the distance across the flats being equal to the diameter of the turning at the thin end.

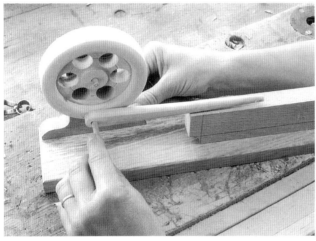

FIGURE 1-12
Try out the movement. If all is well, the flat face of the rod will run smooth against the wheel rim.

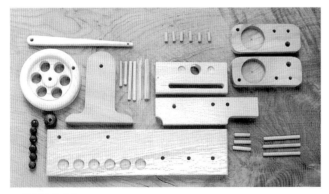

FIGURE 1-13
Check all the component parts out for fit and finish. Make sure mating faces are flush and true.

PUTTING TOGETHER AND FINISHING

1 When you have achieved all the component parts that make up the design, then comes the testing task of getting it all together. You should have eight primary parts in all: the base slab, the stanchion pillar, the flywheel, the piston block, the guide block, the piston, and two guide plates, plus any other bits and bobs that you have the time and energy to make along the way (Figure 1-13).

2 Check the components over, and then use the finest grade of abrasive paper to rub them down to a good finish. Give all the surfaces—barring the mating faces that are to be glued—a swift rub down with a small amount of teak oil.

3 When you are happy with the finish, start by gluing and pegging the stanchion and the guide block to the base board.

4 Glue the dowel in the center of the flywheel, and glue and dowel the guide plates one at either side of a guide block, so that the piston block is nicely contained (Figure 1-14).

5 Set the piston rod in place on the handle dowel, and enter the tapered end into the piston block. Then fit with a glued pin, so that the wooden pin is a tight fit in the block and a loose fit through the rod (Figure 1-15).

6 Test out the movement by slowly turning the flywheel. If all is well, the piston should be at the limit of its run when the rod is fully extended at the quarter-past-the-hour position (Figure 1-16).

7 When you are happy with the movement, then comes the enjoyable task of fitting all the little embellishments that jolly up the design—the turned bead, all the little dowel stubs at the top of the piston, and the half-beads around the circumference of the flywheel.

8 Finally, having first of all waited for the glue to set, give all the surfaces another swift rub down, wipe on another coat of teak oil, and then you can set the wheel turning.

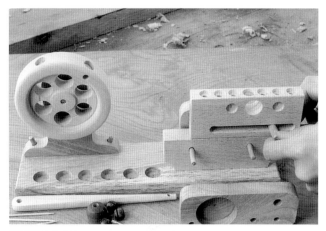

FIGURE 1-14

Fit one guide plate on the guide block, set the piston in place and push the slot dowel in position. You might well need to ease the slot so that the movement is free.

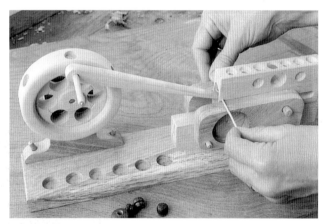

FIGURE 1-15

Push the wooden pin through the piston block and on through the hole at the end of the rod.

PROBLEM SOLVING

■ If you like the overall idea of the project, but want to make something altogether more grand—say much bigger—no problem, as long as you make sure that the diameter of the flywheel, the length of the rod, and the length of the piston block slot are compatible.

■ While I like the project as it stands, Gill reckons that it would be altogether more exciting if we had a set of four flywheels and four pistons, with all the pistons set so that they push one after another. She thinks that it would be more in keeping with the heavy engineering tradition. It sounds so easy!

■ If you like the notion of the project but aren't so keen on woodturning, you could get away with cutting the wheel out on the scroll saw and using a ready made length of dowel for the piston rod.

FIGURE 1-16

If it hangs up when the handle is at the quarter-past-the-hour position, then, chances are, the end of the slot will need to be extended.

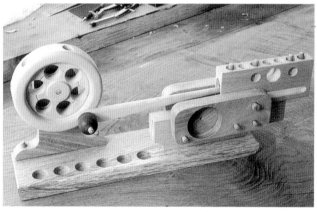

FIGURE 1-17

When you are happy with the fit, then rub the ends of the through-pin down to a flush finish.

■ If the piston block sticks between the guide plates, then try burnishing the sides of the piston with a small amount of beeswax.

■ If the rod is too long to allow the piston block to get to the end of its run, then either shorten the length of the rod or lengthen the guide slot.

■ If you're a beginner to woodturning, then you can take it from me that one of the best extras is the four-jaw chuck. As you can see, it allows you to hold disk blanks securely, without the need for screws.

Differential Pulley Block

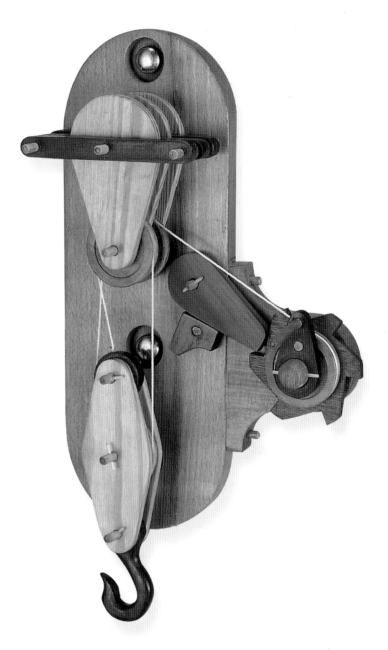

PROJECT BACKGROUND

When we lived by a boatyard, I used to watch in amazement at the launchings. Having spent six months building a wooden fishing trawler that was truly as big as a house—about 60' long with oaken ribs as thick as a man's body, 20' high from keel to deck, all built on top of a massive iron carriage—the builders would use a series of pulleys and levers to inch the finished boat out of the building shed and into the water. They made it look so easy! They'd hook one end of the pulley to the carriage, the other end to one of the huge iron rings set into the quay side. Then they'd pump away at the ratchet handle, and it was beautiful to watch. Four middle-aged men little-by-little inching the big boat from the shed and onto the launching ramp. All of it done with pulleys and levers.

PROJECT OVERVIEW

Look at the project picture to the right, the working drawing (Figure 2-2A) and the design template (Figure 2-2B), and you'll see that the essence of this project is making multiples. There are lots of turned pulleys, wheels, groups of identical plates, sets of holder bars and so on. If you like making repeats, then you are going to enjoy this project.

It's all pretty straightforward, with few critical measurements except for the ratchet wheel. The ratchet is a bit tricky because it must be laid out accurately with a compass. Look at the design template (Figure 2-2B) and note how the wheel design is achieved by scribing radius arcs around the circumference of the circle to divide it up into six equal parts.

This project is designed to be hung on the wall like a picture or a piece of sculpture. The holes in the back board are used as hanging points. What else to say, except that it's a great conversation piece and everything works.

PROJECT TWO: WORKING DRAWING

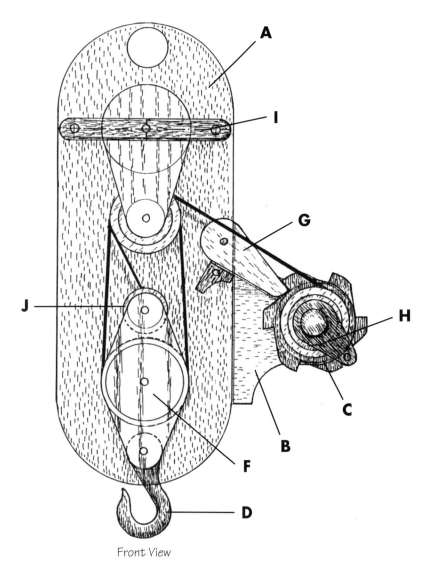

Front View

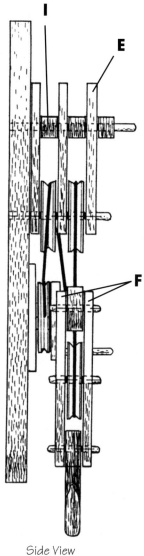

Side View

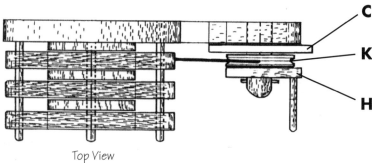

Top View

FIGURE 2-2A

With this project, feel free to experiment with different sizes and thicknesses of wood.

A *Back board*
B *Ratchet outrigger*
C *Ratchet wheel*
D *Hook*
E *Top gang pulley plate*
F *Swinging gang pulley plate*
G *Ratchet stop plate*
H *Handle crank*
I *Holder bar*
J *Distance disk*
K *Pulley wheel*

PROJECT TWO: TEMPLATE DESIGN

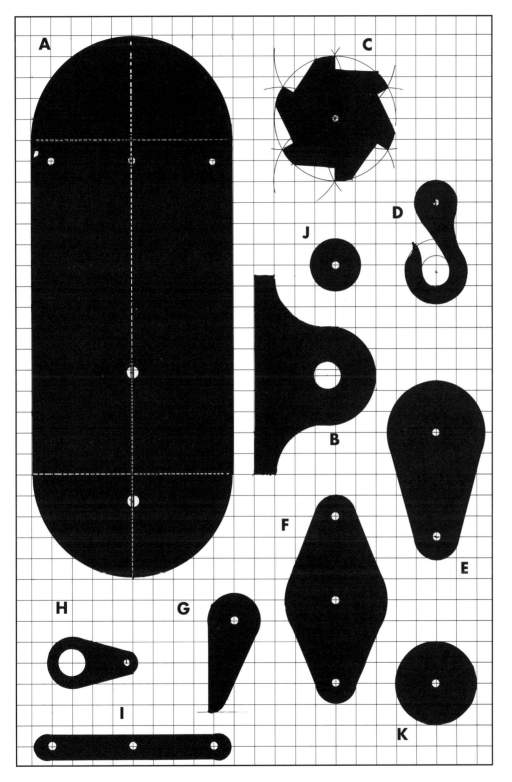

FIGURE 2-2B

The template design at a scale of two grid squares to 1 inch.

A *Back board*
B *Ratchet outrigger*
C *Ratchet wheel*
D *Hook*
E *Top gang pulley plate*
F *Swinging gang pulley plate*
G *Ratchet stop plate*
H *Handle crank*
I *Holder bar*
J *Distance disk*
K *Pulley wheel*

NOTE

As with any wooden sculpture, the dimensions indicated are starting points only. Modify dimensions, spacers and parts as necessary.

CUTTING LIST

Note: All measurements are in inches, and all sizes allow for a generous amount of cutting waste.

Part	Item	Dimensions T W L
A	Back board	¾ x 5½ x 13⅓
B	Ratchet outrigger	¾ x 4 x 5½
C	Ratchet wheel	⅜ x 3½ x 3½
D	Hook	½ x 2 x 3½
E	Top gang pulley plate	⅜ x 3 x 4¾
F	Swinging gang pulley plate	⅜ x 2¾ x 5½
G	Ratchet stop plate	⅜ x 1½ x 3
H	Handle crank	⅜ x 1⅜ x 2⅜
I	Holder bar	½ x ½ x 5
J	Distance disk	⅜ x 1½ x 1½
K	Pulley wheel	A quantity of easy-to-turn wood, 2¾" square

CHOOSING YOUR WOOD

While it's certainly true to say that I always choose my wood with one eye on the decorative appeal, in this instance, certain pieces are primarily chosen for their strength and workability. For example, for the plates I chose pine because it is strong along the run of the grain. For the pulleys I chose beech, because it is both strong and easy to turn. Most important, I chose English plum for the hook, because the hook has to be strong in all directions. Plum is extremely difficult to carve, but the grain is tight and strong making it perfect for the hook. And it looks really good against the bland beech back board.

MAKING THE BACK BOARD AND SIDE RIGGER

1 Check your chosen pieces of wood for problems like knots and splits. Plane all pieces to a finished thickness of ⅝".

2 Study the working drawings carefully, then use a pencil, rule and compass to draw out the two forms for the round-ended back board and the outrigger.

3 Cut these pieces to shape on the scroll saw, then drill the primary holes that make up the design (see Figure 2-2B).

4 When you are happy with the forms, draw in the necessary alignment marks so you know how the outrigger is to be fixed. Then sand them to a smooth finish.

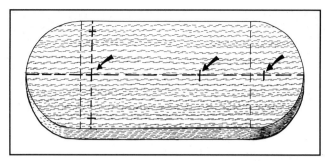

FIGURE 2-3
Set the design out with care, with all center lines in place, so you can establish the precise position of the various pivot points.

MAKING THE PULLEY PLATES

1 First study the drawings (Figures 2-2A&B), noting how there are five plates in all. Three are pear-shaped for the top fixed gang, and two are for the swinging gang.

2 Make sure your wood is absolutely free from splits, and plane it down to a finished thickness of ¼".

3 Again study the drawings, noting how the designs are made up of circles—two for the pear-shaped top plates and three for the bottom plates. Use a compass to draw the designs directly onto the wood.

4 Drill the pivot points with a drill bit that matches your dowel size. Then cut out the shapes on the scroll saw (Figure 2-4).

MAKING THE RATCHET WHEEL

1 Take the wood for the ratchet wheel and plane it down to ¼".

2 Set a compass to a radius of 1½" and mark a 3"-diameter circle on the wood. Then step the radius off around the circumference to divide it into six equal parts. (Note: the circle's radius will be slightly too short to give you six equal segments, so plan on doing some fine-tuning.)

3 Mark straight lines from the six marks on the circumference to the center point. Measure ½" back from the center along each line and make another mark. This allows for the width of the ratchet spurs, cogs and such. There's no problem if your design differs somewhat from mine, as long as the six spurs or cogs on your wheel are all the same shape and size.

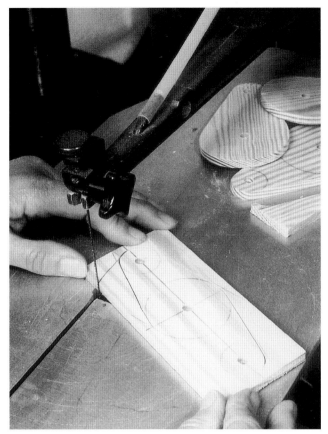

FIGURE 2-4

If you're new to the scroll saw, you might not know that the rate of cut is governed by the speed at which you advance the workpiece. To have more control when cutting tight curves, simply slow down feeding the wood into the blade.

FIGURE 2-5

First cut out the disk, then clear each of the six pieces of waste with two straight cuts.

4 When you're satisfied with the shape, drill a ¾" hole for the pivot and a small hole for the fixing peg.

5 Cut the form out on the scroll saw (Figure 2-5).

MAKING THE HOOK

1 Now comes the good fun of whittling the hook to shape. It's fun because it's also a challenge.

2 Whittling a dense wood like plum is always tough going. The only tricky part is you have to keep changing the direction of the cut as you work around the curves. If you find yourself cutting directly into end grain, turn the hook around and cut from another direction (Figure 2-6).

3 When you have whittled the hook to shape, wrap a fold of sandpaper around a dowel to help you sand the curves. Sand until it's smooth.

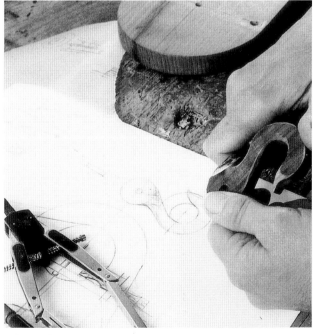

FIGURE 2-6

Work with a controlled paring cut, all the while making sure that you are cutting with the grain.

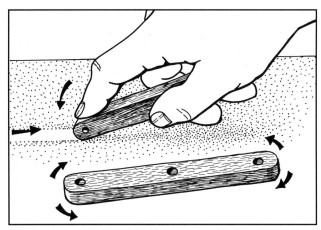

FIGURE 2-7
Roll the sawn ends on the shooting board to make a rounded profile.

FIGURE 2-8
Draw back the tailstock, very carefully skim the leading face of the first wheel to a smooth finish, then wind the tailstock back up so that the wood is supported. Now part the first wheel off. Repeat these steps for each wheel.

FIGURE 2-9
Secure the wheel in the chuck, and use the parting tool to cut the characteristic pulley form.

MAKING THE HOLDER BARS

1 Study the working drawings (Figures 2-2A&B) once again. Notice how you need three holder bars.

2 Plane your wood to a finished thickness of ⁵⁄₁₆", then cut out the three identical bars. Strap them together with masking tape, and drill them with a bit that matches your dowel size.

3 Finally, tidy the curved ends of the three bars with sandpaper (Figure 2-7).

MAKING THE PULLEY WHEELS

1 Take your length of 2¾" square wood, check it for splits and knots—it can't have any—and mount it securely on the lathe.

2 Turn the wood down to a 2"-diameter cylinder. Use the skew chisel to give it a good, smooth finish.

3 Study the working drawings, noting the cross section profile of the pulleys. They should be ⅜" thick with a "V" shape at the center. Take your dividers and mark the cylinder with all the step-offs of this design. Allow ⅜" for each wheel, ¼" for the parting waste, ¹⁄₁₆" for the rim at each side of the wheel, and ¼" for the "V". Repeat the dimensions—¼", ¹⁄₁₆", ¼"—in sequence along the length of the wood. You need five wheels in all: three pulley wheels, one wheel for the ratchet unit, and a fifth wheel for luck in case you make a mistake somewhere along the line.

4 With all the step-offs in place, take the parting tool and remove the waste between each wheel to a depth of about ½", leaving a central core about 1" in diameter.

5 Remembering that each ⅜"-wide wheel has three step-offs (¹⁄₁₆", ¼" and ¹⁄₁₆") and in that order, use the corner of the parting tool to cut the middle (¼") "V" section. Run the "V" down to a depth of about ³⁄₁₆".

6 After cutting the "V" on all the wheels, take the parting tool and, working from the tailstock end, skim the face of the first wheel to a fair finish (Figure 2-8). Then part off the wheel. Repeat for each wheel.

7 When you've finished giving all five pulley wheels a V-groove and one fair face, place them one at a time in the four-jaw lathe chuck and remove the waste until the rim and the central boss stand slightly above the center section (Figure 2-9).

ASSEMBLY AND FINISHING

1 When all the parts have been built—the backing board, outrigger arm, three pear-shaped plates, two diamond-shaped plates, three main pulley wheels, the ratchet pulley, a cogged ratchet wheel, stop lever, winding crank, hook, three holding bars and all the other small pieces (Figure 2-10)—then comes time to put it all together.

2 Check all the parts for problems—splits, rough areas, warping and such. Sand all pieces smooth. Being very careful not to get any on the faces that are to be glued, apply teak oil to the pieces.

3 Start assembly by fitting and gluing the top gang of pulley wheels in place on the back board. The best approach is to fit the plates and the holding bars, and then attach the two pulley wheels (Figure 2-11).

4 Peg and glue the outrigger to the side of the back board. Set the ratchet stop in place on the board, fit the little block that limits the stop, and then glue the ratchet dowel in place (Figure 2-12).

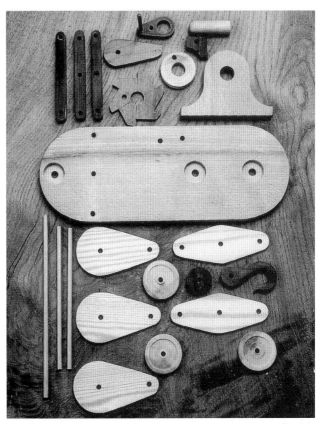

FIGURE 2-10
When you've made all the parts, sand them smooth , clean away the dust and then apply a small amount of teak or Danish oil. Keep the oil off the faces that will be glued.

FIGURE 2-11
Be careful when gluing the dowel. Only glue the plate holes, so the wheels are free to move.

FIGURE 2-12
The little dark block under the ratchet stop is a limiter. It keeps the stop from dropping down.

FIGURE 2-13

Smear glue on all mating faces of the ratchet unit—the ratchet, pulley wheel, crank and the little holding dowel. You want the three components to move as one.

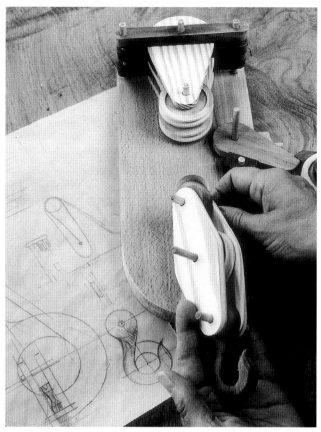

FIGURE 2-14

All three components need to be free moving within the plates.

5 The fitting order for the ratchet unit on the dowel is: cogged ratchet, pulley wheel, crank, hold peg and handle dowel. A small peg through the dowel holds everything in place (Figure 2-13).

6 The swinging gang—the unit with the single pulley wheel and hook—is wonderfully easy to fit. All you do is sandwich the hook, pulley and spacer wheel between the two plates, then glue the dowel pivots in place. Keep the glue at the end of the dowels so the three components at the center of the sandwich are free to move (Figure 2-14).

7 To install the drive cord, follow this road map: start at the top spacer wheel on the swinging gang, go over and around the front pulley on the top unit, then down to the pulley on the swinging unit, back up to the back pulley on the top unit, and then finally round to the pulley on the ratchet unit. Fix the ends of the cord by gluing them into pegged, drilled holes (Figure 2-15).

PROBLEM SOLVING

■ Depending on your choice of drive cord, you may need to make the V-section grooves on the pulley wheels slightly deeper.

■ We relied on a four-jaw chuck to make these parts. If you don't have one, you'll need to either purchase one or work in a way that suits your lathe setup.

■ In retrospect, Gill reckons that this project would have been more successful if we had made everything much smaller. You might want to build this at half the listed size.

■ When you come to fitting the ratchet wheel, you may find it necessary to use pencil, paper and a piece of cardboard to determine the precise position of the stop and block.

The Excentric Squirrel Fan

PROJECT BACKGROUND

The excentric squirrel fan is a mechanism designed to draw in and compress large volumes of air using centrifugal force. If you want to ventilate a ship, factory, a mine shaft, or push warm air from one room to another, then this is the fan to use. In use, the air is sucked in through small vents at the sides, compressed during its progress through the spiral and then forced out from the outlet mouth, with each wing of the fan acting as a valve. As to why it's called an "excentric squirrel" fan, I can't say for sure, other than this is the term and the spelling that was used by a certain Sir John Robinson, in 1850 or thereabouts, when he designed a revolutionary new warming and ventilating arrangement for his house in Edinburgh, Scotland. The spelling for "excentric" is weird but correct.

PROJECT OVERVIEW

Have a look at the project picture above, the working drawings (Figure 3-2A) and the template designs (Figure 3-2B). The fan is made up from a backing board, a frame plate and a base board, with the three components sharing the same profile. This was achieved by sandwiching three boards and then cutting them out all of a piece—with the resultant waste being used for a good number of the other components. The movement is achieved by means of a drive belt that runs from one wheel to another, with the motive force being supplied by the crank handle. The good fun thing with this project is not so much the smooth movement of the fan, but rather the fun is in the making. I say this, because to my mind, there is something particularly pleasuresome about the procedure of cutting and fitting the fan wings so that they are a tight close fit within the frame plate.

PROJECT THREE: WORKING DRAWING

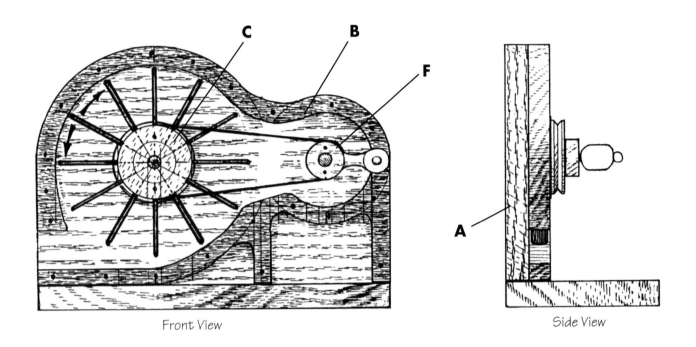

Front View

Side View

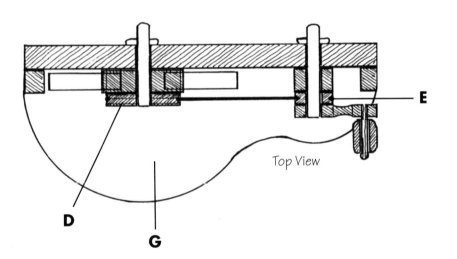

Top View

FIGURE 3-2A
- **A** *Backing board*
- **B** *Frame plate*
- **C** *Fan hub*
- **D** *Hub belt wheel*
- **E** *Small belt wheel*
- **F** *Crank handle*
- **G** *Base board*

FIGURE 3-2B

The template design at a scale of two grid squares to 1 inch.

A *Backing board*
B *Frame plate*
C *Fan hub*
D *Hub belt wheel*
E *Small belt wheel*
F *Crank handle*

NOTE

As with any wooden sculpture, the dimensions indicated are starting points only. Modify dimensions, spacers and parts as necessary.

CUTTING LIST

Note: All measurements are in inches, and the sizes allow for a generous amount of waste. The sizes of the small parts aren't listed because they are cut from the waste necessarily left over after cutting the primary components.

Part	Item	Dimensions T W L
A	Backing board	1 x 7 x 10
B	Frame plate	1 x 7 x 10
C	Fan hub	Cut from waste
D	Hub belt wheel	1½ x 2½ x 2½
E	Small belt wheel	Cut from waste
F	Crank handle	½ x 1¼ x 2½
G	Base board	1 x 7 x 10

CHOOSING YOUR WOOD

Though the choice of wood is pretty straightforward in terms of technique—no complex procedures that require specific wood types—you do still have to spend time making sure that there is a good contrast from one component part to another. After thinking long and hard about the various possible combinations and permutations, I decided to have the back board and the base board cut from the same wood, with the frame plate and most of the other component parts being cut from wood of a contrasting color. At the end of it all—after searching through my wood pile and generally counting costs and looking at sizes—I went for pine for the backing board and the base, mahogany for the frame plate and the wheels, and odds and ends for the rest. Note how the project starts with three boards being sandwiched and cut all of a piece. It's worth saying here, that I never ever buy new endangered wood—like mahogany—I either use wood salvaged from the sea or from some long gone item of broken furniture, or I do without and use a renewable species. My wood came from the sea—probably the seat plank from a yacht.

MAKING THE BASE, BACK AND FRAME BOARDS

1 Having first studied the working drawings and the template designs (Figures 3-2A&B), take your chosen wood for the base, back and frame, and plane the three boards to a finished thickness of ⅝".

2 Set the three boards together in a sandwich—in the order from bottom to top, base, back and frame—and tap small panel pins through the corners of waste.

FIGURE 3-3
Cut out the form, so that you have three identical profiles.

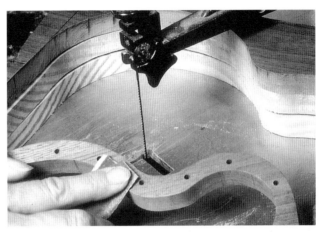

FIGURE 3-4
The top profile is further worked on the scroll saw, so that you are left with the frame. Don't cut across the large areas of waste because you will need them for the other component parts.

3 Draw the design of the frame out on the top board.

4 When you are clear in your own mind as to the order of things, move to the scroll saw and carefully fret out the outer profile. At this stage, you should finish up with three identical profiles (Figure 3-3)—same shape on both the under and top sides.

5 Take the frame profile and continue working on the scroll saw until you have achieved the characteristic form.

6 Sit the frame plate on the backing board, drill the pattern of fixing holes, and then—being very careful not to split the wood along the fragile short grain—use a fold of sandpaper to clean up.

MAKING THE FAN WHEEL

1 Take the wood that you have chosen to use for the fan hub and then use the compass fixed at a radius of a little under 1⅛" to draw out a circle with a radius of 2⅛". Draw an inner circle at about 1" diameter.

2 Run a hole through the center of the drawn out circle to match up with the diameter of your chosen pivot dowel.

3 With the compass still set at the radius measurement, first step off around the circumference so that you have six equal divisions, and then halve the divisions so as to divide the circumference into twelve equal parts, like the face of a clock.

4 Draw lines from the circumference intersections to the center—just like the spokes of a wheel—and then move to the band saw and run straight saw cuts along the spoke lines, stopping short at the line of the inner circle.

5 Lastly, move to the scroll saw and cut around the outer circle so that you finish up with the hub wheel (Figure 3-5).

6 Take the wood for the wing flats and plane it down to a thickness of about 1/16". Cut the wood into twelve identical lengths at a little under ½" wide and 1⅞" long.

7 One piece at a time, take a small sharp knife and shave away the thickness at one end, until it is a tight push fit in the band saw cut (Figure 3-6).

MAKING THE BELT WHEELS

1 Having first used a plane to thickness your chosen wood to ⅜", then use the compass to set out the two circles—1⅞" diameter for the large wheel, and ¾" for the small one.

2 Cut the two circles out on the scroll saw.

3 One blank at a time, take the knife and the riffler file and cut and work the V-groove (Figure 3-7). Run three pencil lines around the thickness of the wood so that you have four bands—two equal outer bands at ⅛" and two inner side-by-side bands at 1/16". Run a stop-cut down between the two 1/16" bands, and cut into the stop-cut to make the V-section. Do this on both wheels.

FIGURE 3-5
First cut the slots and then cut out the circle. This way of working allows you to correctly align the band saw cuts well before they enter the circle.

FIGURE 3-6
Shave the wood on both sides so that each wing is a tight push fit. If you are using a hefty saw blade or thin veneers, then you could maybe miss out on the shaving stage.

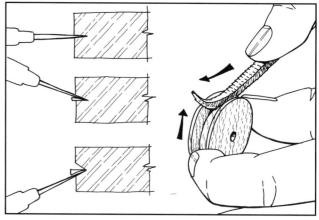

FIGURE 3-7
Use a knife to cut the V-groove, then run the riffler file over and round—always working with the run of the grain.

FIGURE 3-8
Work with a tight paring stroke—as if you were paring a small apple.

FIGURE 3-9
Sand the peg to a round section so that it's a loose fit through the knob and a tight fit in the crank hole.

MAKING THE CRANK HANDLE

1 Plane the chosen wood to a thickness of about ⅜".

2 Run a center line down the width of the wood so that it is aligned with the direction of the grain. Then use the compass, rule and pencil to set out the design.

3 With a drill bit to match the diameter of your dowel, run holes through the two pivot points. Then fret the profile out on the scroll saw.

4 Use the penknife to whittle the arm of the crank to a round section finish. Work from end to center so as to avoid running the blade into end grain (Figure 3-8).

5 Having made the knob—I turned mine, but you could just as well use a found bead—take a little scrap of easy-to-carve wood and make a little pivot pin to run through the knob (Figure 3-9). Work the whittling with a knife and fine grade sandpaper, until it is a tight fit in the crank and a loose fit through the knob, with the swelling at the end of the pivot acting as stop.

PUTTING TOGETHER AND FINISHING

1 Take all the component parts and check them over for possible problems—pay particular attention to the fan hub. See how I trimmed back the width of my base board by about 2", so that it looks more balanced. When you are happy that all is correct, then comes the time to a have a trial run putting together.

FIGURE 3-10
The frame plate might well warp when it has been cut. If this happens, then you will need to ease it to fit.

FIGURE 3-11
Trim the wings on both sides, and set them in the slots so that they are in alignment with the radius lines.

2 Position the face frame plate on the backing board and mark its position. Establish the precise position of the two wheel pivots, and run them through with a bit size to match your chosen dowels.

3 Set the frame plate in position on the back and run selected fixing holes through the thickness of the back board. Fix the frame with three or four cocktail-stick pins (Figure 3-10).

4 Set the wing flaps in the hub slots, and make adjustments (Figure 3-11) until the total diameter of the fan makes for a tight fit within the frame plate.

5 Place the drive belt wheel on the top face of the hub, and fix it with wooden pins (Figure 3-12).

6 Once the fan wheel is in place, drill the rest of the holes through the base board. If your frame warped, you might need to fiddle around for best fit (Figure 3-13).

7 Slide the spacer wheel on the drive pivot (Figure 3-14), and then fit the crank and wheel unit.

8 Take a waxed twine and cut and knot a two-strand drive belt to fit.

9 Finally, disassemble the components and work through the usual procedures of fine sanding, oiling, gluing and waxing.

PROBLEM SOLVING

■ One of the biggest difficulties with this project is choosing the wood for the fan wings. Not only do you need a wood that is straight grained, with a lot of strength along the run of the grain, but the wood must be relatively easy to plane. I chose ash, but you could just as well go for beech, maple or some types of pine. You could even buy ready-cut veneers and sandwich them to make the thickness.

■ Be very careful when you are cutting the frame plate that you don't break the form across the short grain.

■ Use wax-lined cord for the drive belt, or even one of those little track belts from a child's construction kit.

■ When you are working the V-section wheels with the riffler file, you will need to change your approach to suit the run of the grain. For example, if you arrange your disk blank so that the grain runs from 6 o'clock to 12 o'clock, then you will have to work up and down from 3 o'clock and 9 o'clock.

FIGURE 3-12
The belt wheel is best fixed in place with a couple of pegs—the idea being that you then don't have to worry so much about the fitting at the gluing stage.

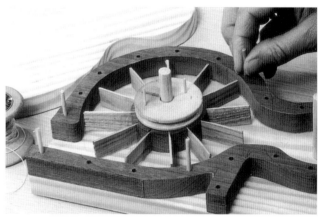

FIGURE 3-13
The frame might need to be repeatedly eased to fit.

FIGURE 3-14
It's important that the spacer stand slightly proud of the frame plate so that the crank handle is lifted fractionally clear of the frame.

Steam Crank Slider Mechanism

Instructions for building this project begin on page 9.

Differential Pulley Block

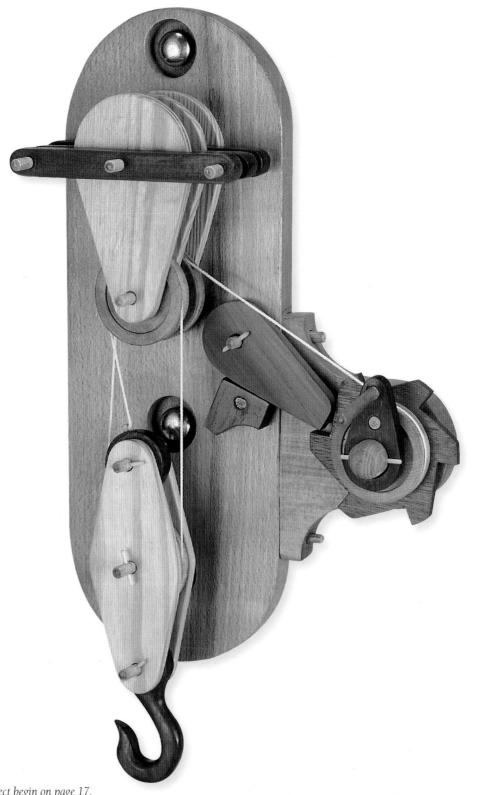

Instructions for building this project begin on page 17.

The Excentric Squirrel Fan

Instructions for building this project begin on page 26.

Six Valve Radial Engine

Instructions for building this project begin on page 46.

Wheel & Worm Gear Mechanism

Instructions for building this project begin on page 54.

Film Advancing Mechanism

Instructions for building this project begin on page 62.

The Universal Joint

Instructions for building this project begin on page 70.

Camshaft Valve

Instructions for building this project begin on page 78.

Water Lift Pump

Instructions for building this project begin on page 86.

Lever & Ratchet Mechanism

Instructions for building this project begin on page 93.

Screw Jack

Instructions for building this project begin on page 101.

The Bicycle Chain Machine

Instructions for building this project begin on page 110.

The Wonderful Wilmhurst Machine

Instructions for building this project begin on page 118.

Six Valve Radial Engine

PROJECT BACKGROUND

I have to admit that I am not an engineer. I know something about pumps and pulleys, and I'm very interested in wind power, motorcycles and all manner of old machines. But when it comes to sophisticated items like the six valve radial engine, I'm in the dark. Maybe I ought to explain.

When I see an engine, all stripped down and oily, I don't see it in terms of valves, pistons and gears, but rather as a mechanical sculpture. I don't need to know that such and such an engine comes from a 1999 Chevy or a 1961 Jaguar or whatever; my pleasure is seeing how the shapes of the pistons, valves and cranks fit together and move. To me it's pure joy to watch as one movement is converted into another. So when I first saw a working model of an early radial engine in a museum, I was excited by the sheer beauty of the mechanical motions.

PROJECT OVERVIEW

Study the project picture above, the working drawing (Figure 4-2A) and the template design (Figure 4-2B). More than anything else, this project is about working on the lathe. Just about everything is turned. Plus, you need a four-jaw chuck and should be pretty confident in your woodturning skills.

The building process is not so much tricky, or even difficult, as it is finger-knotting and time consuming. If you have a lathe, enjoy turning, your skill level is high and you have a plenty of patience, then you are going to have a lot of fun building this project.

PROJECT FOUR: WORKING DRAWING

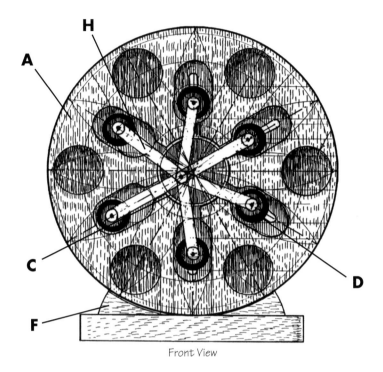

Front View

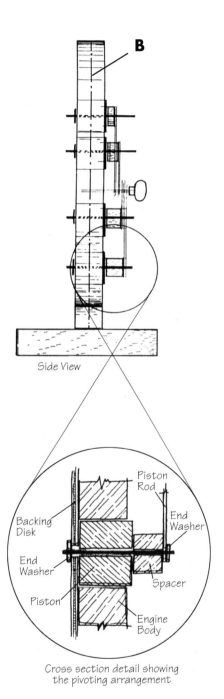

Side View

Cross section detail showing
the pivoting arrangement

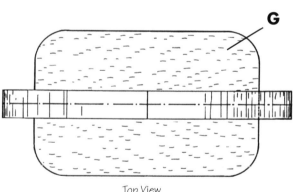

Top View

FIGURE 4-2A

A *Engine body*
B *Backing disk*
C *Crank disk*
D *Pistons*
E *Spacers*
F *Base mounts*
G *Base slab*
H *Piston rods*

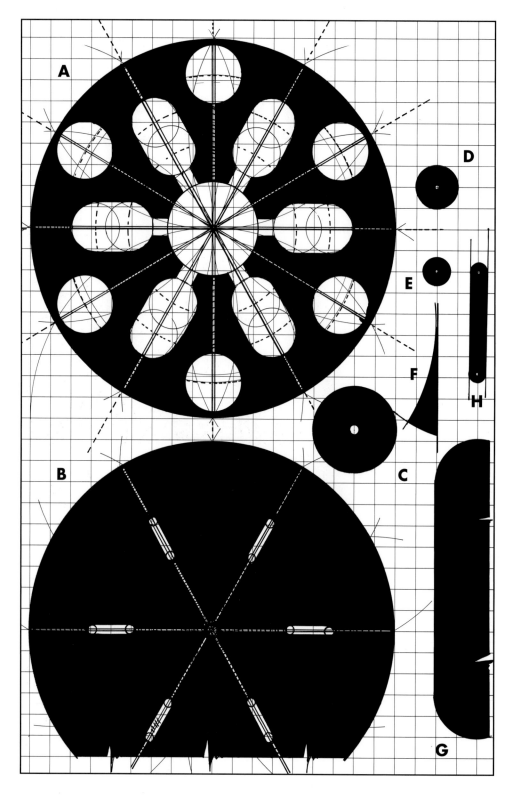

FIGURE 4-2B

The template design at a scale of two grid squares to 1 inch. Note with the engine disk, how the design is based on a hex form, with the step-offs being established by making radius arcs.

A *Engine body*
B *Backing disk*
C *Crank disk*
D *Pistons*
E *Spacers*
F *Base mounts*
G *Base slab*
H *Piston rods*

NOTE

As with any wooden sculpture, the dimensions indicated are starting points only. Modify dimensions, spacers and parts as necessary.

CUTTING LIST

Note: All measurements are in inches, and the sizes allow for a generous amount of waste.

Part	Item	Dimensions T W L
A	Engine body	1¼ x 10 x 10
B	Backing disk	⅛ x 10 x 10
C	Crank disk	1¼ x 2½ x 2½
D	Pistons	1½ x 1½ x 1½
E	Spacers	½ x 1 x 1
F	Base mounts	Offcuts of beech
G	Base slab	1 x 5 x 7½
H	Piston rods	3⁄32" thick

CHOOSING YOUR WOOD

The choice of wood is governed almost entirely by technical need. The wood needs to be easy to turn and strong. For these reasons, I chose lime for the main engine body, thin plywood for the backing disk, beech for the base and the side mounts, a dense African walnut for the pistons and plum for the piston rods. The pieces that pose the most challenge are the piston rods. The wood for these needs to be strong even when it's cut into thin slices.

MAKING THE BASE

1 Take the 1"-thick slab of wood for the base and plane it down to a finished thickness of ¾".

2 Use a square, rule and compass to lay out the design on the wood, then cut it to shape on your scroll saw.

3 Sand it to a smooth finish.

4 Cut the two little mount wedges to shape and size, so the top curve is a partial circle that comes from a circle with a radius of 4½" (Figure 4-3).

MAKING THE ENGINE BODY

1 Take your 10"x10" slab of wood and draw crossed diagonals to find the center point. Set your dividers to a diameter of 4¾" and scribe a 9½"-diameter circle.

2 Use a 2¼"-diameter Forstner bit to drill through the center of the blank.

FIGURE 4-3

Set the wedges to the base so that the part-circumference curves fit a 9"-diameter disk.

FIGURE 4-4

The whole procedure of turning the engine disk is made easy by the use of a four-jaw chuck. You will need to turn the jaws around so that the steps fit inside the hole at the center of the circle, so that the jaws grip when they are wound apart.

3 Change the jaws of your lathe chuck so they're in the expanding mode. Mount the disk on the lathe and turn it down to size: ⅞" thick and 9" in diameter (Figure 4-4).

4 Turn the finished disk over in the chuck. Cut a guide line around the circle about ⅛" in from the edge, then lower the face of the resulting 8¾" diameter circle to a depth of ⅛" or the thickness of the plywood you're using. The idea is to fit the plywood disk into the recess so it's contained.

5 With your compass set at a radius of 4½", make six equal step-offs around the circumference. Then use the six points to draw in all the details of the design (see Figures 4-2A&B).

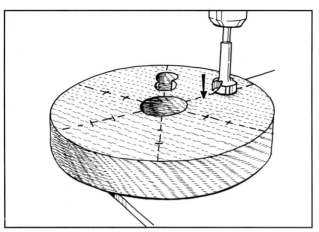

FIGURE 4-5
You need to sink two holes for each piston chamber—one at each end of the chamber.

FIGURE 4-6
Use a slightly heavier blade to saw the edges of the piston chambers so that the sawn faces are at right angles to the face of the disk.

6 Use a 1³⁄₁₆"-diameter Forstner bit to drill out the piston chamber holes (Figure 4-5). Drill two holes for each chamber.

7 When you have marked out the design and drilled out the ends of the piston chambers, use a scroll saw to cut out the rest of the design (Figure 4-6). Make sure the sawn edges are clean and crisp and at right angles to the face of the disk.

8 Finally, use progressively finer grades of sandpaper to get a smooth finish. Pay particular attention to the sides of the piston chambers (Figure 4-7).

FIGURE 4-7
Spend a good time sanding all the sawn faces to a good smooth finish. Make sure that all the edges are slightly rounded—especially the edges of the chamber holes.

MAKING THE BACKING DISK

1 On the plywood, draw a circle that matches the turned recess, and cut it out on the scroll saw.

2 Study the working drawing, noting how the slots on the plywood disk relate to the movement of the piston centers. Using a pencil, rule and compass, mark the position of the slots. Make the slots slightly wider than the diameter of your piston-center dowels.

3 Cut the slots out on the scroll saw. The best way is to drill two holes in each of the drawn slots, one at each end. Detach the saw blade and pass it through the hole, reattach and tension the blade, then cut out the slot (Figure 4-8). Remember to drill a hole through for the crank disk pivot.

4 Finally, sand all the sawn edges to a smooth finish. Do a trial fitting in the recess, sanding until everything fits properly.

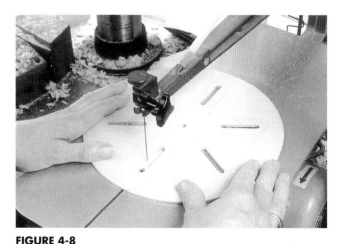

FIGURE 4-8
The best way of establishing the position of the slots is to draw the shape of the chambers through from the engine disk. If you follow this course of action, then you must put alignment marks on both components so that you can correctly fit them back together.

MAKING THE PISTONS AND SPACERS

1 With the engine body complete, take the wood you chose for the pistons and check that it's free from splits and knots.

2 Set the square wood section in the lathe and turn it down to a cylinder with a diameter that is slightly smaller than the width of your piston chambers. For example, if your chambers are 1³⁄₁₆" wide, then make a cylinder that's 1" or 1¹⁄₁₆".

3 Using dividers make alternate step-offs ¼", 1", ¼", 1" and so on along the length of the wood until you have seven 1" pistons marked. (Six you know you need and one extra for luck.)

4 Mark the wood and the chuck so you know how it fits in the lathe. Then take it off and see how the cylinder fits in the chambers (Figure 4-9).

5 Remount the workpiece, and turn it down to a good fit. Part off the pistons by bringing the leading face of the first piston in line to a good finish, removing the waste so the piston falls free. Wind the tailstock center in so that the wood is once again supported, face up the next piston, and so on down the line. If all is well, the pistons should be a nice fit and stand above the face of the engine body by about ³⁄₃₂" (Figure 4-10).

6 When you have made all the pistons, make the spacer disks in like manner. The only difference this time around, is that the disks are about ⅝" diameter and made so that they range in multiples of the thickness of the piston rods. That means if your piston rods are ³⁄₃₂" thick, then the first disk needs to be ³⁄₃₂" thick; the next one twice ³⁄₃₂" (that would be ³⁄₁₆"); the next three times ³⁄₃₂" (⁹⁄₃₂"); the next four times ³⁄₃₂" (⅜") and so on (Figure 4-11).

7 Finally, part the spacers off as described for the pistons, and drill them through with holes to match your piston dowels.

MAKING THE CRANK DISK

1 Study the working drawing and the template design. Note the relationship between the movement of the pistons within their cylinders and how the length of the rods governs the precise position of the crank hole on the crank disk. Draw your disk to size accordingly, aiming for a tight but smooth fit.

FIGURE 4-9
The piston needs to be sized so that when it is fitted it stands slightly proud of the face of the engine disk.

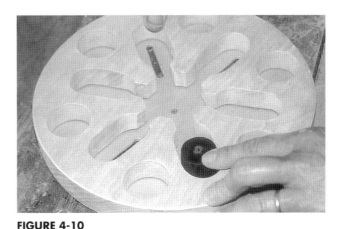

FIGURE 4-10
Try the piston out for size. If the fit is close and you need to adjust the chambers, then be sure to number the pistons and the chambers so that they match.

FIGURE 4-11
The spacers are vital to the smooth running of the machine, so spend time making sure that they are all correctly sized.

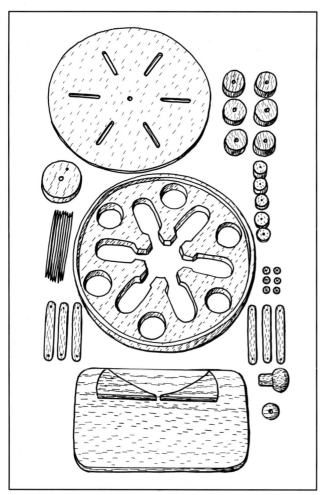

FIGURE 4-12
Gather all the component parts and check them over for problems. Make sure that mating surfaces are smooth to the touch and free from rough corners and edges.

2 Plane the wood to thickness, and cut the disk out on the scroll saw.

3 Drill two holes—one at the center for the main pivot dowel, the other one about ⁷⁄₁₆" out from center for the crank rod.

MAKING THE RODS AND PISTON WASHERS

1 Take your carefully selected wood—I chose plum—and plane it down to a thickness of ³⁄₃₂".

2 Lay out the rod dimensions on the wood. They should be about ⅜" wide and the holes centered about 2½" apart. The exact measurements should come from your specific parts.

FIGURE 4-13
Check the rod for size—make sure that the piston doesn't stick in its chamber—meaning when the crank pin is furthest away from the piston.

3 Cut the rods to size on the scroll saw, then strap them together with masking tape so you have a little bunch. Drill the two holes through all the pieces at once.

4 Use the same thickness of wood for the washers. Cut the washers to size at about ½" diameter, then drill to suit. You need twelve washers in all, six for the front of the machine and six hidden away at the back.

5 Thread the twelve washers on a piece of wire or toothpick and sand them until they're smooth and crisply rounded.

ASSEMBLY AND FINISHING

1 Group all the component parts and check them for fit and finish. It may help you to number the parts and draw in alignment marks. Wipe on a small amount of teak oil (Figure 4-12).

2 Glue and pin the plywood disk in place in the recess at the back of the engine disk. Set the crank disk in place, and then put the six pistons into their chambers (Figure 4-13).

3 Run the small diameter rods through the pistons, and set the spacers in place. The assembly order around the engine disk is: no spacer, thinnest spacer, next thinest spacer and so on, with the number six spacer the thickest. Set the crank rod in place in the crank disk, and start placing the piston rods (Figures 4-14, 4-15).

FIGURE 4-14
Fit the rods in sequence so that they are parallel and aligned to the face of the engine disk.

FIGURE 4-15
If the rod looks to be a little short, then be ready to sand the chamber so that it's slightly longer.

4 Set the turning handle in place and test the movement (Figures 4-16, 4-17). You may have to ease the holes a bit until the movement is smooth.

5 When you've fitted the rods in an ascending spiral, mark what goes where and how.

6 Finally, when you are sure everything is properly in place and up and running, glue the whole works together. Set the engine disk on its stand, burnish the moving parts with a small amount of beeswax to reduce friction, and the job is done.

PROBLEM SOLVING

■ If you find the movement sticking, then you might need to shift the position of the crank disk pivot hole. If this is the case, then it's a good idea to drill a line of holes so you have choice of holes.

■ If you're unsure how something works and the components relate to each other, it's a good idea to make a working model. It's easy enough to make a flat desktop model from cardboard.

■ The piston rollers need to be made from a dense, heavy hardwood, ideally one that has an oily finish.

■ Finding good quality small-diameter dowels is always a problem. I tend to use a mix of cocktail sticks, barbecue sticks and kebab skewers.

■ Be sure to wax moving parts before you assemble the machine, to cut down on the friction.

FIGURE 4-16
Note how piston number one doesn't need a spacer.

FIGURE 4-17
Test out the full movement before you lift the whole works up, and fit the washers to the ends of the through-piston pins.

Wheel & Worm Gear Mechanism

PROJECT BACKGROUND

The wheel and worm gear mechanism is a device for "cross-axis movement"—a device for changing the direction of the movement while at the same time changing the gear ratios. In this instance, the speed of the fast-turning worm gear is converted into a slow-turning wheel. If you really enjoy techno-babble, worm gears provide the simplest means of obtaining large ratios in a single pair. Such mechanisms are used when the axes for transmitting motion are not in the same plane.

Just in case you're more a sculptor-woodworker than a mechanical engineer, what this means is that the screw zooms around while the wheel creeps. It's a fascinating mechanism to watch in action. It is beautiful, almost hypnotic.

PROJECT OVERVIEW

Study the project picture at left, the working drawing (Figure 5-2A) and the template design (Figure 5-2B). For the most part, this project has to do with careful lay-out, precise work on the scroll saw and painstaking whittling. Note how the mechanism is made up of two primary parts: the large wheel with all the teeth and the turned cylinder or shaft with the carved worm. In action, the crank handle turns easily in one direction while the wheel slowly turns in another. While the building steps are all pretty easy, it's fair to say that cutting the worm takes a lot of finicky patience. That said, this is one of those beautiful, juicy projects that—once the basic sawing and turning are out of the way—can be quietly worked on out on the porch or in the garden.

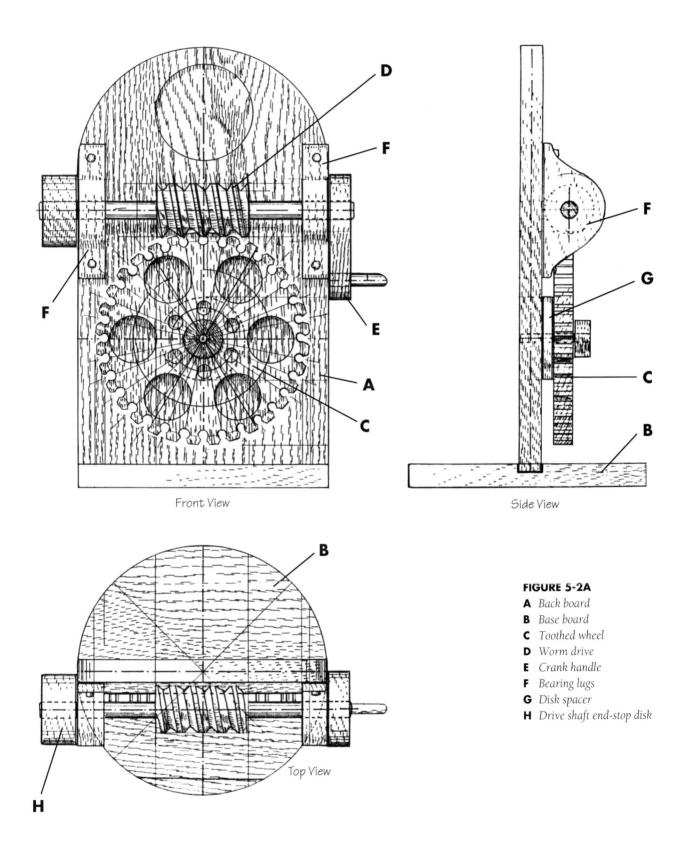

Front View

Side View

Top View

FIGURE 5-2A
A *Back board*
B *Base board*
C *Toothed wheel*
D *Worm drive*
E *Crank handle*
F *Bearing lugs*
G *Disk spacer*
H *Drive shaft end-stop disk*

PROJECT FIVE: TEMPLATE DESIGN

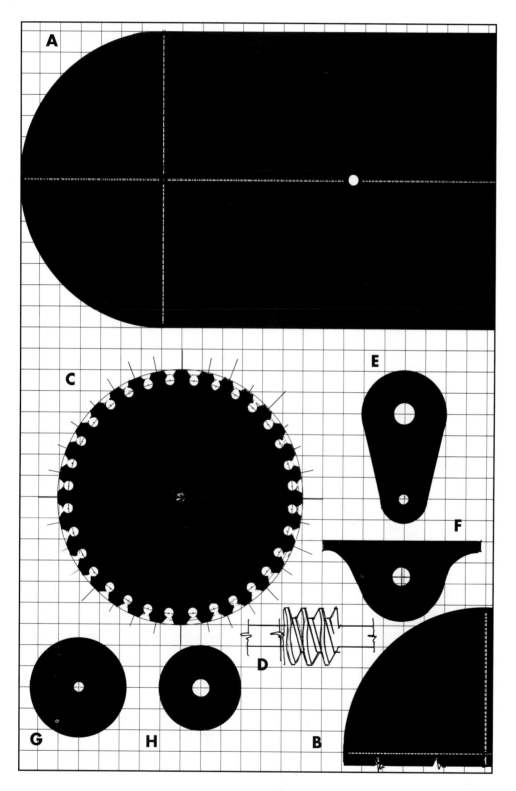

FIGURE 5-2B

The template design at a scale of two grid squares to 1 inch.
A *Back board*
B *Base board*
C *Toothed wheel*
D *Worm drive*
E *Crank handle*
F *Bearing lugs*
G *Disk spacer*
H *Drive shaft end-stop disk*

NOTE

As with any wooden sculpture, the dimensions indicated are starting points only. Modify dimensions, spacers and parts as necessary.

CUTTING LIST		

Note: All measurements are in inches, and the sizes allow for a generous amount of waste.

Part	Item	Dimensions T W L
A	Back board	¾ x 7½ x 12½
B	Base board	¾ x 7½ x 7½
C	Toothed wheel	¾ x 7 x 7
D	Worm drive	2 x 2 section at least 10" long
E	Crank handle	¾ x 2½ x 4
F	Bearing lugs	¾ x 2 x 4½
G	Disk spacer	⅜ x 3 x 3
H	Drive shaft end-stop disk	1¼ x 2¼ x 2¼

CHOOSING YOUR WOOD

When choosing your wood, remember: The wheel must be strong across the run of the grain so it can be sawn and pared without crumbling, and the worm must be both easy to turn and easy to carve. Taking these considerations into account, and having first dug into my mountain of scrap pieces, I opted to use oak for the wheel, pine for the back and base boards, cherry for the bearing lugs, lime for the worm and whatever happened to fall to hand for the other parts.

MAKING THE BACK AND BASE BOARDS

1 Study the working drawings (Figures 5-2A&B) so you understand how the project needs to be

FIGURE 5-3
Using a combination plane is a great swift and easy way of cutting the housing channel. Note the setup that allows the plane fence to run clear of the edge of the bench.

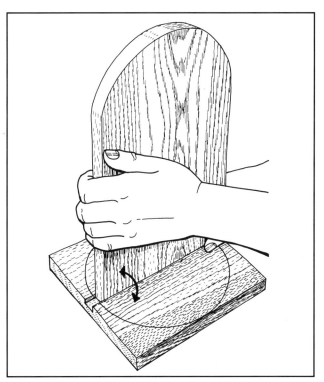

FIGURE 5-4
Make sure that the boards are a good tight fit and at right angles to each other.

worked and put together. Plane your wood for the back and base board down to a finished thickness of ⅝".

2 Use a compass to draw the 6"-diameter circle to make the base and the half-circle that goes to make the back board. Complete the design with a rule and square. Cut the back board out on your scroll saw.

3 Use the tools of your choice to run the ⅝"-wide housing channel across the base. I used an old combination plane (Figure 5-3), but you could just as well use a saw and chisel or a router.

4 Work the channel until it takes the back board for a nice tight push fit (Figure 5-4). When you're happy with the joint, cut the base disk out on the scroll saw.

MAKING THE WHEEL

1 Having planed your chosen wood to a finished thickness of ⅝" and drawn and cut out the 6"-diameter blank, use a protractor, square and a compass to lay out the design of the teeth. Lay out a 5½" circle on the 6"-diameter blank, then divide the circle into 64 equal segments. Mark the intersection of every other point. You should end up with 32 center points about ⅜" in from the circumference of the blank.

2 When you are satisfied with the arrangement of the teeth, use a compass to lay out the position of the various holes that make up the decorative design.

3 Move to the drill press and drill a ¼"-diameter hole through every other intersection, so you have alternating holes and spaces running around the circle. A total of 32 holes and 32 spaces.

4 Using both the holes and the guidelines as an aid, draw out the shape of the teeth using a pencil and rule.

5 When you're sure all is correct, move to the scroll saw and very carefully cut out the shape of the teeth (Figure 5-5). For me, the best procedure was to work each tooth in turn—two straight cuts in toward the center point of each hole.

6 When you've cut out the basic profile, take a razor sharp knife (or you may prefer a chisel) and pare the teeth to a slightly rounded finish (Figure 5-6). Be watchful that you don't cut directly into end grain.

7 Finally, put the wheel on a rod, and see how it looks from various angles and when it's turning (Figure 5-7).

MAKING THE WORM

1 Make sure your square section length of wood is free from splits and awkwardly placed knots. Look especially for end splits that darken as they run up the length of the grain. If you have any doubts at all, reject the wood and find another piece.

2 Mount the wood on the lathe, and use a gouge to swiftly turn it down to a 1⅝"-diameter cylinder. Keeping in mind that it's important the turning be crisp and smooth, switch to the skew chisel and skim the cylinder down to a finished size of 1½".

3 Use a rule and the point of the skew chisel to lay out the central stepped area on the cylinder. I divided the length of the wood in half and put the 2½"-long step-up at the center.

4 Use the gouge to turn the wood at each side of the central step-up to a finished diameter of about ½". You should finish with the shaft ½" in diameter to each side of center, and the central area 1½" in diameter and 2½" long (Figure 5-8).

FIGURE 5-5

It's important that the cuts be clean and at right angles to the face of the wood. It's a good idea to fit a new blade, adjust the tension and make sure that the table is set at 90° to the blade.

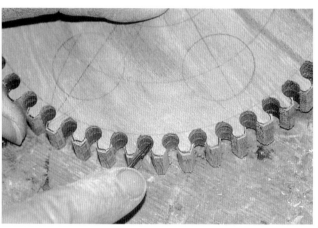

FIGURE 5-6

Be sure, when you are tidying up with the knife or chisel, that the workpiece is arranged so that you are cutting with the grain. It's a good idea to work on a smooth surface or a work board.

FIGURE 5-7

Make yourself a jig so that you can test out the movement. All you need is a vertical surface with a pivot hole—the edge of the bench, a piece of waste, anything will do.

FIGURE 5-8
Though I spent some considerable time humming and haring over my choice of wood, I still came across a small knot—see just right of the cylinder. Fortunately, it doesn't get in the way of things.

5 Study the working drawings (Figure 5-2A) and the template designs (Figure 5-2B), then use a combination square with a protractor head (or a similar tool) to lay out the angle of the worm (Figure 5-9). Although it looks a little complicated, the point to remember is that the windings of the worm as they wrap around the shaft must be spaced so that they fall naturally between the teeth of the wheel. If the tooth V-section centers are about ½" apart, then the top peaks of the worm also need to be about ½" apart.

6 With the guidelines in place, take a sharp knife and run a stop-cut around the cylinder, centered between the worm peaks.

7 Make the stop-cut to a depth of ⅛", then make slicing cuts at an angle at each side so you have a V-section furrow running around the wood (Figure 5-10). The band at the top of the worm should be about ⅛" wide.

8 Continue in this way, repeatedly making the stop-cut deeper, slicing down at each side into the stop-cut at an angle until you've created the characteristic worm profile (Figure 5-11).

9 Try out the wheel on a jig, turning the worm over by hand so the wheel makes a full revolution without sticking. Use fine grade sandpaper to rub the whole worm down until it's smooth.

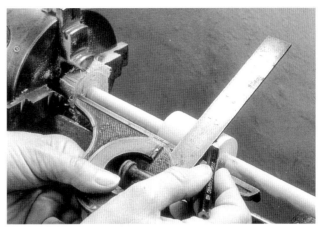

FIGURE 5-9
Note the protractor square—the perfect tool for the task—picked up for pennies on a junk market.

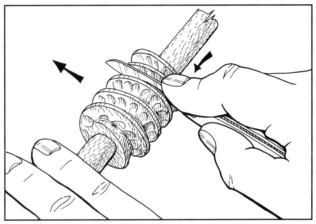

FIGURE 5-10
Repeatedly run and roll the blade in the V-furrow so as to cut a stop-cut guide for subsequent cuts.

FIGURE 5-11
Remove the waste by sliding the blade down at an angle into the stop-cut. Do your best to keep the ⅛"-wide band at the top of the peak.

FIGURE 5-12
Check the components out for problems—especially the worm drive and the wheel. It's vital that all the teeth are intact—no splits or knots.

FIGURE 5-13
At a later stage, the dowel can be fitted by being cross-drilled and pinned with a cocktail stick.

FIGURE 5-14
The little strip of waste prevents the top of the dowel from being crushed and damaged.

ASSEMBLY AND FINISHING

1 Lay out all the component parts (Figure 5-12) and check them over for potential problems. Make sure that the wheel is free from splits, with all the teeth intact, and the worm drive is as near perfect as you can make it.

2 Don't worry at this stage about the final finishing of the other parts. It's much more important to make sure the movement is going to work properly. Set the wheel in place on the back board (the assembly sequence is back board, spacer disk and wheel) with the dowel pivot pushed through from the front (Figure 5-13).

3 Set one lug bearing in place, slide the worm drive shaft through the bearing so the worm is aligned in the teeth of the wheel. Then fit the other lug bearing (Figure 5-14).

4 With the worm drive centered, slide the stop disk and the crank handle onto the shaft and bring them up to the lugs. Keep in mind that it's the proper placing of these two components that determines the position of the worm and the subsequent smoothness of the movement (Figure 5-15).

5 Set the back board in the base channel and check it over for fit (Figure 5-16).

6 Finally, when you're happy with the way all the components come together, disassemble the whole works, do a finish sanding of all surfaces, wipe over with teak oil (but not the surfaces being glued), glue up and polish.

FIGURE 5-15
Spend time getting the spacing right, and then draw in alignment marks.

PROBLEM SOLVING

■ If you have any doubts as to how the design of the wheel is laid out, then work it out on paper before doing anything to the wood.

■ Another way to pinpoint the position of the 64 divisions: draw the circle out on paper with a compass. Draw a line dividing the circle in half, then quarters, and so on, dividing each angle until you have 64 divisions. Then cut the circle out and use it as a template in marking the wood blank.

■ The choice of wood for the worm is critical. It's got to be smooth grained and easy to carve. My first choice is European lime.

FIGURE 5-16
If you have got it right, the handle can be wound in either direction.

Film Advancing Mechanism

PROJECT BACKGROUND

This beautiful little mechanism perfectly illustrates the action inside some old-time movie cameras—when, as a frame is shot, a claw moves on its eccentric drive pivot and pulls the film down one notch. It's good fun to watch the machine in action. When the handle is turned, the arm moves up-round-and-in, the claw at the end of the arm engages in the notch, the notched component is dragged down, the claw disengages, and the counterbalance weight pulls the notched component back up into the ready-to-go position. Of course, if you like the notion of springs or elastic bands or whatever, then you can do away with the counterweight and change the working action accordingly. And just in case you have a mind to go delving into your modern camera to see if you can find such a mechanism (so that you can push and poke it around and maybe even watch it in action), I would strongly warn against it. I did just such a thing at the start of the project, and I have got to tell you—if I'm lucky, my camera will be back from the repair shop some time in the new millennium. In my camera, the mechanism is much changed—it's minute, no bigger than the lower-left side whisker on a small gnat.

PROJECT OVERVIEW

Have a look at the project picture on this page, the working drawing (Figure 6-2A) and the design template (Figure 6-2B). See how the challenge of this project has to do not so much with making the various components (after all, most of them are easily fretted out on the scroll saw) as it does with putting the whole works together. All that said, it's important to note that the relationship between the length of the crank and the position of the various pivot centers is critical. If you make a mess-up of one or all of these details, then you can expect the action to fail. Best advice with this project is to make a card prototype flat down on a board—with thick card and thumb tacks—and fix the critical measurements before you ever get to cutting the wood. Note that the large disk at middle right acts as a distance piece or spacer to keep the clawed arm on course.

PROJECT SIX: WORKING DRAWING

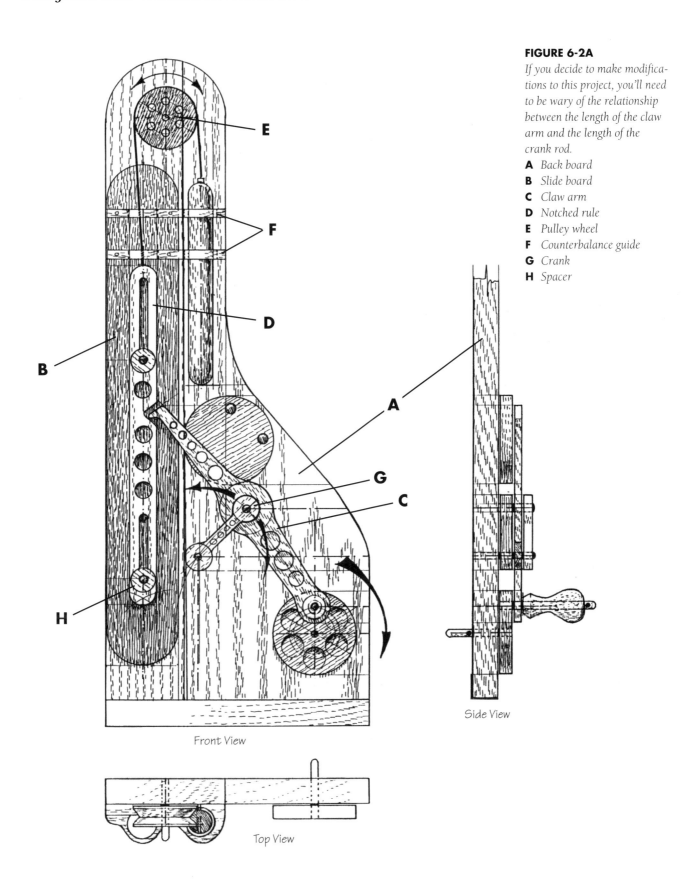

FIGURE 6-2A

If you decide to make modifications to this project, you'll need to be wary of the relationship between the length of the claw arm and the length of the crank rod.

A *Back board*
B *Slide board*
C *Claw arm*
D *Notched rule*
E *Pulley wheel*
F *Counterbalance guide*
G *Crank*
H *Spacer*

Front View

Side View

Top View

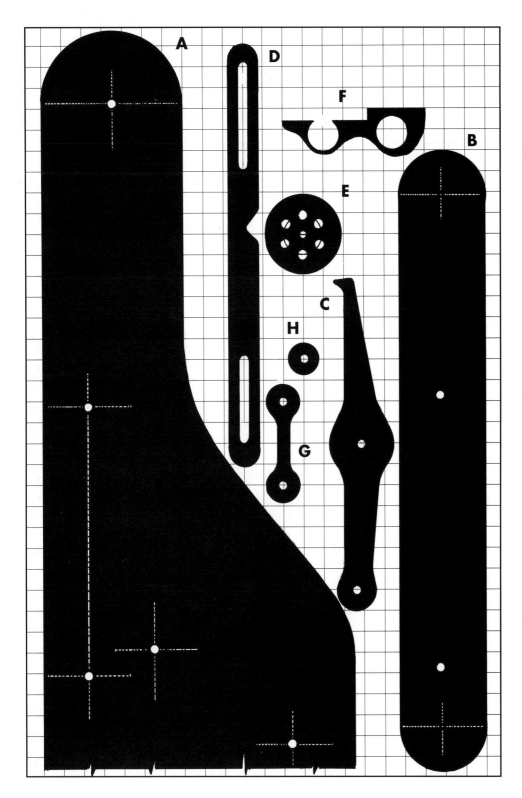

FIGURE 6-2B

The template design at a scale of two grid squares to 1 inch.

A *Back board*
B *Slide board*
C *Claw arm*
D *Notched rule*
E *Pulley wheel*
F *Counterbalance guide*
G *Crank*
H *Spacer*

NOTE

As with any wooden sculpture, the dimensions indicated are starting points only. Modify dimensions, spacers and parts as necessary.

CUTTING LIST

Note: All measurements are in inches, and these sizes allow for a generous amount of waste.

Part	Item	Dimensions T W L
A	Back board	1 x 8 x 20
B	Slide board	½ x 3 x 15½
C	Claw arm	⅜ x 2 x 8
D	Notched rule	⅜ x ⅞ x 11
E	Pulley wheel	¾ x 2 x 2
F	Counterbalance guide	⅜ x 1½ x 4
G	Crank	⅜ x 1 x 3
H	Spacer	⅜ x 1 x 1

CHOOSING YOUR WOOD

Since most of the components are cut out on the scroll saw, and the mechanical movement is delicate and controlled, you can use just about any wood you like. Just make sure it's easy to saw and stable, with no warping, cracks or loose knots. I chose pine for the base, back board, the notched slider and the balance guide; oak for the claw arm; a scrap of mahogany for the wheels, and odd bits of scrap for the other parts. The counterbalance weight is made from the heaviest wood I could find, a chunk cut from an old, broken walking stick.

MAKING THE BASE AND BACK BOARDS

1 Study the designs, the working drawings (Figure 6-2A) and the template designs (Figure 6-2B). Then plane the wood to a finished thickness of ¾".

2 Use a compass and rule to draw the back and base board designs on the wood. Cut the profiles out on a scroll or band saw.

3 Make a cardboard prototype so you know the precise positions of the various critical pivot points. Transfer this information to the back board, and drill a hole that matches your dowel pivots. Check and double-check the centers (Figure 6-3).

MAKING THE CLAW ARM

1 First study the working drawings (Figure 6-2A), noting how the position of the centers and the claw are critical—exactly 3½" between centers and 3⅞" between the crank center and the end of the claw.

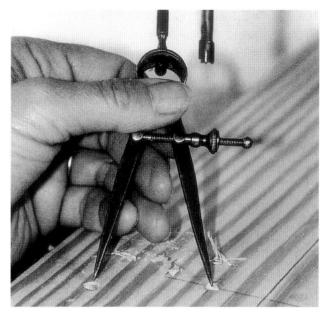

FIGURE 6-3
Check the center points with a pair of dividers. It's vital that they are well placed.

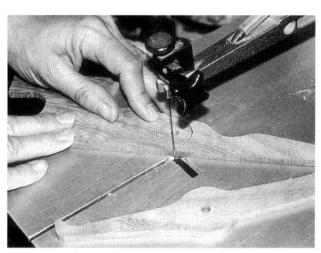

FIGURE 6-4
If you go at the sawing nice and easy—with a new blade and the correct tension—you will finish up with a cut edge that is so smooth that it hardly needs to be sanded.

2 Plane the wood to a finished thickness of ¼". Use a rule, compass and straight edge to lay out the design. There's no problem if you want to change the profile so long as you stay with the critical measurements just described.

3 When you are happy with the design, drill the centers with a bit that matches your dowel pivots, and cut the form out on your scroll saw (Figure 6-4). As long as you're at the saw, cut out the spacers and the various disks.

MAKING THE NOTCHED RULE

1 Study the working drawings, then plane your wood to a finished thickness of ¼". Draw the design onto the best face.

2 Run a center line down the width of the profile, and use it as a guide to mark the position of the two slots and the notch.

3 Drill the holes through on a drill press, and cut the slots out on a scroll saw. The procedure for cutting the slots is to first drill pilot holes at the ends of both slots, detach the top end of the blade from the scroll saw and pass it through the pilot hole, reattach the blade and re-tension. Cut out the slot, then detach the blade once again (Figure 6-5). It's easy enough, the only real trick is using a new blade and adjusting the tension until the blade "pings" when strummed. Be sure to cut a little to the waste side of the drawn line.

MAKING THE COUNTERBALANCE GUIDE BRIDGES

1 Study the working drawings (Figure 6-2A), noting how the two guides are set together in such a way that they contain the counterbalance weight, keeping it from moving sideways and forming a channel for the cord. The outer profile of the guides can be just about any shape and size that catches your fancy, so long as the counterbalance holes fit the shape and size of your balance.

2 Since the guides are relatively fragile, drill the holes through before cutting the profile on the scroll saw (Figure 6-6).

DRILLING HOLES

1 The easiest way to drill the various holes is using a drill press and Forstner bits (Figure 6-7).

2 Use a ruler and dividers to establish the position of the various holes, mark the centers and then drill the holes through (Figure 6-8). You also need to drill some blind holes—holes that don't go all the way through the wood—so be sure to set the drill stop to the required depth.

MAKING THE PULLEY WHEEL

1 Plane your wood to a finished thickness of ⅜", then adjust your dividers to produce a 1⅞"-diameter circle. Draw the circle onto the wood, and with the

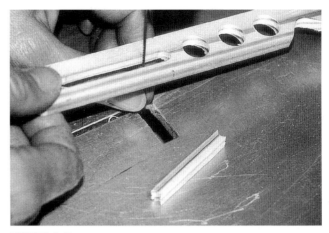

FIGURE 6-5
The slot needs to be worked to fit both your chosen dowel diameter and the size of your drill bits.

FIGURE 6-6
The grain at either side of the bridge is short and fragile—go at it easy.

FIGURE 6-7
Set the depth stop so that the blind holes are all the same depth.

FIGURE 6-8
The blind holes are purely decorative—they draw their inspiration from the forms that you see on old cast iron machines.

FIGURE 6-9
Always cut in the direction of the grain—meaning from the rim and down towards the bottom of the stop-cut.

compass still set at the radius measurement, strike six arcs around the circumference. Use these intersections to establish the centers of the six decorative circles.

2 Cut the disk out on the scroll saw.

3 Take a sharp knife, run a stop-cut around the thickness of the wood, and then, little by little, slice in at either side of the stop-cut until you have a V-section channel running around the circumference. To do this, run the blade around the disk so as to cut a stop-cut in to a depth of about ⅟₁₆", then work around the disk making angled cuts that run into the stop-cut so that chips of waste fall away. Then tidy up the shallow "V", and make another stop-cut. Then repeat the procedure. And so you continue—cutting and slicing until you have what you consider is a good V-section groove (Figure 6-9).

4 Drill out the seven holes that go to make the design—the central pivot hole that runs through the thickness of the wood, and the six blind holes. Plug the six holes with short stubs of dowel made from a contrasting wood—to give the wheel a rivet effect (Figure 6-10). If you cut the dowel with a sharp knife—by rolling the blade over the dowel—you will find that you finish up with stubs that are nicely rounded at the ends.

5 It's a good idea at this stage to rub the face of the wheel down to a good finish, and then glue the stubs in place—so that they don't get mislaid (Figure 6-11).

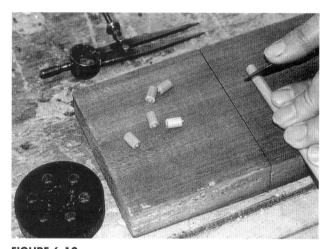

FIGURE 6-10
Use a heavy rolling action to cut the stubs. Note that the use of a level board ensures that the rolled cut runs true—to start and finish at the same place.

FIGURE 6-11
Rub the face of the wheel down to a good finish, and glue the stubs in place.

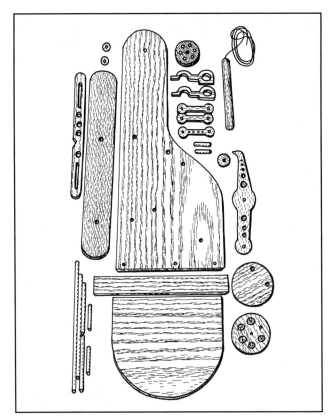

FIGURE 6-12
Check the component parts off against the working drawings. If you have doubts about what goes where and how, then it's a good idea at this stage to pencil label each part on its underside.

ASSEMBLY AND FINISHING

1 Lay out the parts and make sure they're free from splits, loose knots and warping (Figure 6-12).

2 Now comes the exacting task of doing a dry fit assembly. Start by dry doweling the slide board to the back board.

3 Take the notched rule and plug the cord into a hole drilled into the top end with a small length of toothpick (Figure 6-13). Plug the other end of the cord into the counterbalance weight.

4 Set the notched rule in place in the slide board, and fit the two stop dowels so they go through and into the back board (Figure 6-14). These dowels have a dual function. They hold the components together and create stops that control the up-and-down movement of the notched rule.

5 Set the various wheels in place—the pulley wheel, handle crank wheel (Figure 6-15) and the large spacer disk.

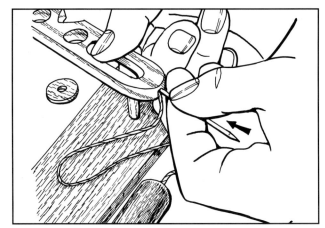

FIGURE 6-13
Push the cord into the hole and wedge it in place with a cocktail stick.

FIGURE 6-14
Fit the dowels and the washers so that there is nice smooth movement between mating parts.

FIGURE 6-15
Set the crank wheel in place on its dowel. Note that when it comes to the final fixing, the dowel will need to be glued into the wheel and loose fixed through the backing board.

FIGURE 6-16
Fit the two bridges with wooden pins and then label them so as to avoid a mix-up.

6 Fit the two guide bridges with small lengths of toothpick. The guides need to be parallel to each other and square to the slide board, with the stepped part of the guides pressing hard up against the edge of the slide board (Figure 6-16).

7 Proper cord movement over the pulley wheel is critical. If the V-groove is too sharp, pinching the cord, or the dowel is too tight so the wheel doesn't turn, then now is the time to fix things.

8 When you fit the crank rods, be sure you have the slightly thicker rod on the underside. This is because the underside rod, the slide board and the large spacer disk are all the same thickness.

9 Once the crank rods have been installed so the claw arm is nicely contained, then pivot the handle through both the lower end of the claw arm and the crank wheel. The important thing here is that the pivot dowel must be flush with the face of the wheel. This allows the claw arm to pass over the pivot without obstruction (Figure 6-17).

10 When you test the movement, you may have to slightly trim back the tip of the claw and/or slightly modify the shape of the notch. You will almost certainly need to tweak one or all the parts to achieve a smooth movement.

11 When you're satisfied with the movement—be picky—then disassemble the whole works. Sand all faces and edges smooth, rub oil on the parts except where glue will be applied, and then glue up.

FIGURE 6-17
Note that when it comes to the final fixing, the cranks need to be glued to the dowels, with the claw arm and the back end of the top dowel being a loose easy fit.

PROBLEM SOLVING

■ The biggest problem I had was making sure the thickness of the various layers was uniform, as this is essential to smooth movement. The best way of ensuring uniformity is cutting the crank wheel, bottom crank, disk spacer and the slide board all from the same piece of wood.

■ The notched rule needs to be a smooth-working fit. It's a good idea to wax the mating faces before final assembly.

■ You may find the claw arm warping slightly, so the claw bends back and butts up against the edge of the slide board. The fix is to make a more stable claw arm by building it up from several laminations.

The Universal Joint

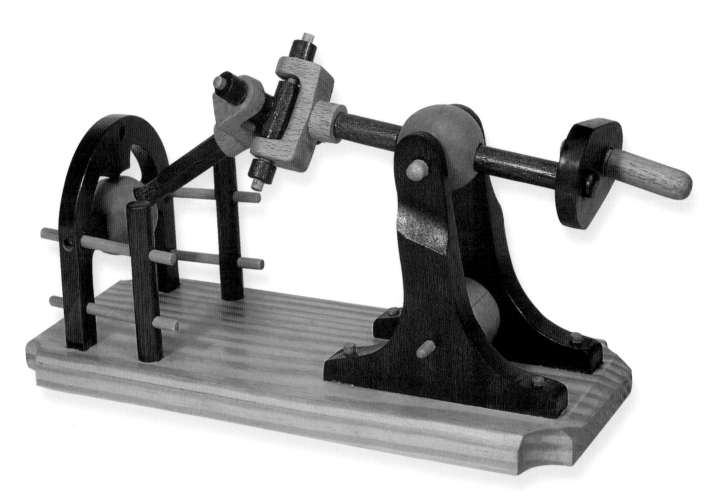

PROJECT BACKGROUND

This mechanism beautifully illustrates the action of the common U-joint or universal joint. You'll find these on the drive shafts of all automobiles. In engineering terms, the universal joint is used to transmit power from one shaft to another over varying angles. It's a simple solution to what was once a difficult mechanical problem, and our current wide array of vehicles wouldn't exist without them.

PROJECT OVERVIEW

Study the project picture above, the working drawings (Figure 7-2A) and the design template (Figure 7-2B). Note how our wooden machine replicates a universal joint from the underside of a car. Imagine the handle as the engine and the bridge stanchion as the back axle end. You'll see how, even though the engine and the axle wobble up and down independently, the universal joint still allows the two shafts to keep turning. Note how the action of the shafts as they pass through the split ball joints allows them to change in length as the angle varies.

This is a complex project that's both tricky to make and just as tricky to fit together. So before you begin, thoroughly study the working drawings and details.

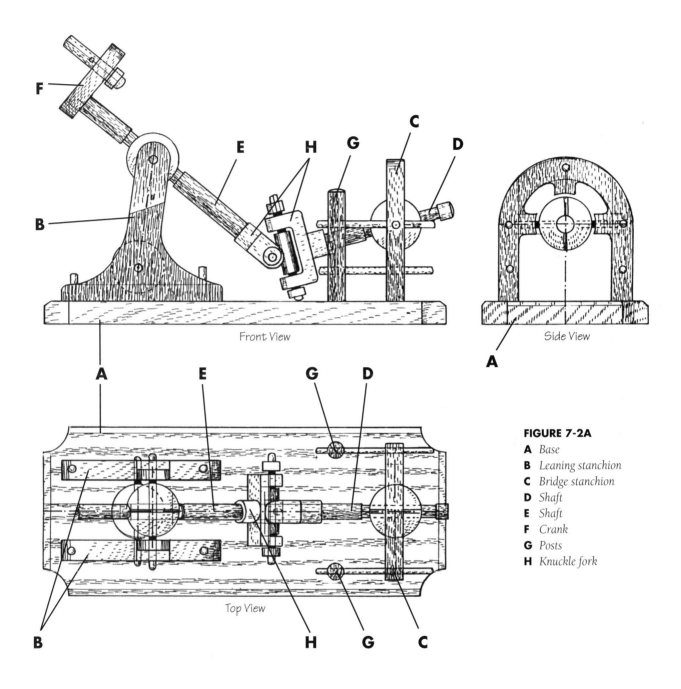

Front View

Side View

Top View

FIGURE 7-2A

A *Base*
B *Leaning stanchion*
C *Bridge stanchion*
D *Shaft*
E *Shaft*
F *Crank*
G *Posts*
H *Knuckle fork*

PROJECT SEVEN: TEMPLATE DESIGN

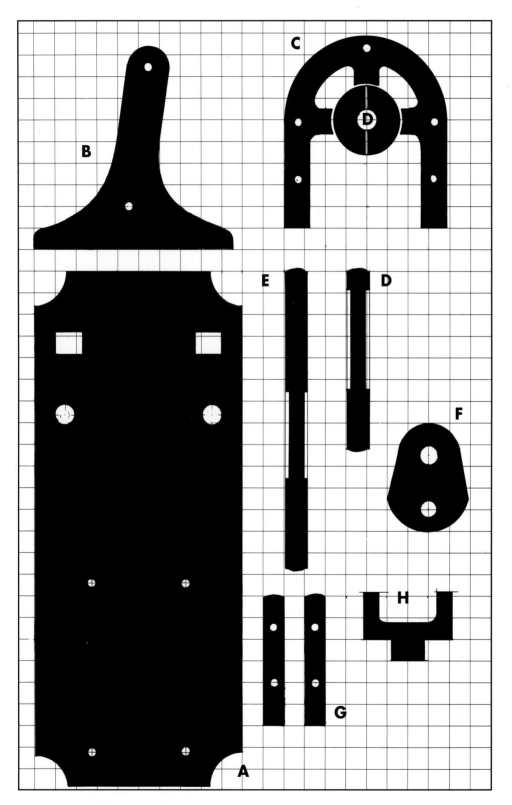

FIGURE 7-2B

The template design at a scale of two grid squares to 1 inch.

A *Base*
B *Leaning stanchion*
C *Bridge stanchion*
D *Shaft*
E *Shaft*
F *Crank*
G *Posts*
H *Knuckle fork*

NOTE

As with any wooden sculpture, the dimensions indicated are starting points only. Modify dimensions, spacers and parts as necessary.

CUTTING LIST

Note: All measurements are in inches. The sizes allow for generous cutting waste. Sizes relate to single components.

Part	Item	Dimensions T W L
A	Base	1 x 6 x 13
B	Leaning stanchion	¾ x 6 x 6
C	Bridge stanchion	¾ x 5 x 5
D	Shaft	½" diameter
E	Shaft	½" diameter
F	Crank	¾ x 2½ x 3
G	Posts	½" diameter
H	Knuckle fork	1 x 2 x 2½

FIGURE 7-3
Take the squared up partial sawn unit and run it through with the coupling pivot holes and the shaft hole—with bit sizes to suit the diameter of your chosen dowels.

CHOOSING YOUR WOOD

There are many factors that determine the choice of wood. The balls must be easy to turn on the lathe, the bridge needs to be strong across short grain, and the universal joint must be strong across the prongs. A search through my scrap bin produced pine for the base, American oak for the knuckle forks, a hardwood dowel for the shafts, English plum for the bridge stanchion, mahogany for the two leaning stanchions, lime for the turned balls and whatever was at hand for the secondary components.

MAKING THE KNUCKLE FORKS

1 Plane your wood for the two knuckle fork components down to a finished thickness of ¾".

2 Study the template designs (Figure 7-2B), noting the shape of the knuckle in that view, and then draw the same view out on the face of your planed wood.

3 Partially cut the fork shape out on your scroll saw—cut just the shape at the shaft-face end. Then use a pencil and rule to mark the position of the various centers—the center on the shaft-end and the centers for the coupling pin. Establish the center of the shaft-end face by drawing crossed diagonals.

4 Use a compass to draw in the circle at the shaft-end and the curves at the ends of the prongs. Then move to the drill press and use a ½" bit to drill the shaft hole to a depth of about ½", and a ¼" bit for the couplings holes. The coupling hole should be drilled completely through the wood (Figure 7-3).

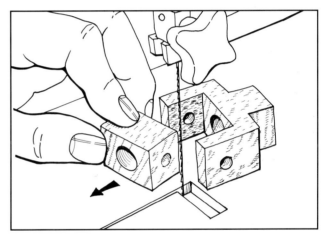

FIGURE 7-4
Complete the cutting on the scroll saw.

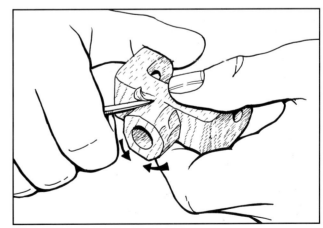

FIGURE 7-5
Use a knife to whittle the curves that go to make up the design—the ends of the prongs and the shaft. Run the blade in the direction of the grain so as to avoid cutting into end grain. Whittle down to the shoulder line into the stop-cut.

5 When the holes are in place, finish cutting the form out on your scroll saw (Figure 7-4).

6 Once you have the basic form, whittle out the various curves that make up the prongs of the fork and the round shape of the shaft socket. To make the shaft, make a stop-cut around the shoulders of the fork, and then, little by little, skim down the shaft and into the stop-cut until you are down to the shoulder line (Figure 7-5).

MAKING THE CROSS-COUPLING UNION

1 Use a knife to cut three lengths of ½" dowel for each fork. One dowel piece should fit loosely between the prongs, the other two shorter pieces at each end of the coupling pin. Roll the dowel under the knife so the cut ends are nicely formed.

2 Using a bit size that matches the pin diameter, drill through the dowel lengths. Then check to see how the components fit together (Figure 7-6).

3 Take the two longer dowel pieces, measure along the length to find the centers, and use a small knife to cut a little recessed "flat" on each length. Cut the flats until the two dowels mate together, forming a right-angle cross (Figure 7-7).

4 Glue the two pieces of dowel together, creating the cross coupling. Then take the knuckle forks and push a length of ½" dowel into the shaft holes. Cut the coupling dowels either flush or leaving a bit sticking out as I did, and then do a trial fitting. If you've got it right, you should be able to hold the shafts at just about any angle and spin them with the joint happily turning to match the changing angles (Figure 7-8).

MAKING THE STANCHIONS

1 Look at the working drawings (Figure 7-2A) and you'll see there are three stanchions—the two leaning post stanchions at the handle end and the single bridge at the other end. With all three, the grain needs to run vertically when cut.

2 Plane the wood to thickness of about ⁷⁄₁₆" for the bridge and ⅝" for the stanchions.

3 Take the two leaning post stanchion pieces and sandwich them together with pins in the waste or double-sided tape.

FIGURE 7-6
Have a trial fitting with the coupling tube and the rings. Note how the little radius curves help to create an image that looks as if it has been cast—like part of a machine.

FIGURE 7-7
Cut flats so that the two units mate together at right angles. Be careful not to cut through to the pivot hole.

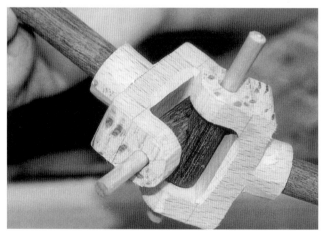

FIGURE 7-8
Spin the shafts and see how the coupling rolls into action.

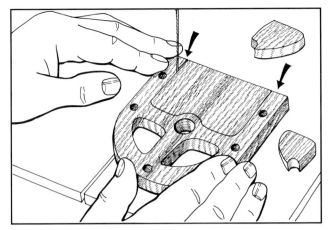

FIGURE 7-9
Pay particular attention to the last ½" or so of the legs that need to be tenoned into the base.

FIGURE 7-10
Cut the mortises to fit the legs, and then pencil label one or both so that you know what goes where. Note the way that the shaft has been necked with a stop at the end.

4 Draw the designs of the stanchions onto all three pieces (the two leaning post pieces and the bridge stanchion). Drill the necessary holes through the bridge, then cut the profiles out on your scroll saw (Figure 7-9). Take extra care when you're cutting the legs of the bridge, keeping the cuts crisp and clean.

5 Carefully cut away half the thickness on the top outside face of both leaning stanchions—about an inch or so.

6 Sand the pieces smooth.

MAKING THE BASE

1 Plane the base slab wood to a finished thickness of about ¾".

2 Plane one edge square, then use the square, rule, pencil and compass to lay out the design on the wood. The base will be 5"x12", with the corner curves having a radius of ¾". Draw a center line down the length.

3 Cut out the base. Then use a block plane to miter the edges on the top face, ends and sides. Cut the corners out on your scroll saw.

4 Finalize the position of the components on the base—the bridge, the two leaning stanchions and the various posts—marking their location.

5 Drill the posts and dowel peg holes. Use a small bevel-edged chisel to cut the blind mortise holes. Cut the holes little by little to a depth of about ¼", until the legs of the bridge are a tight push fit (Figure 7-10).

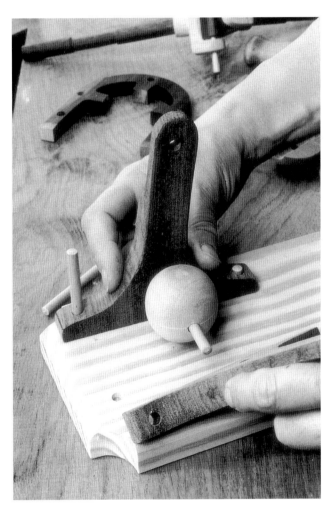

FIGURE 7-11
The bottom ball functions in much the same way as a stretcher under a chair, meaning it helps brace and distance the two stanchions.

FIGURE 7-12
Run the dowels through the stanchion and on into the ball—to stop just short of the shaft.

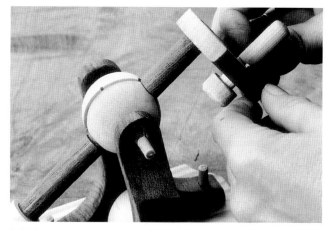

FIGURE 7-13
Fit the crank and the handle on the end of the shaft, and check out the movement of the handle.

ASSEMBLY

1 Turn, drill and slice the balls in half—see other projects in this book for details on turning the balls. Take all the parts and check them over for fit, finish and potential problems. Don't worry at this stage about final finish sanding, as we're first going to do a trial assembly.

2 Start by fitting the two leaning stanchions. Fit and peg the spacer ball between the two stanchions, then set the whole works on the center line and peg the feet of the stanchions through the base slab (Figure 7-11). Make sure that the stanchions are leaning in towards the slab.

FIGURE 7-14
Use the point of a knife to slide the grub dowel into place.

3 Whittle a section of the shaft so that it's a good sliding fit between the halves of the sliced pivot-ball. Then run pegs through the stanchions and into the ball so the shaft is contained and the ball pivots nicely (Figure 7-12).

4 Set the crank plate on the end of the shaft, then cut and fit the handle from scrap wood. I used a length of dowel for the handle, with a ring pushed onto the end and a wooden peg run through to keep the whole thing in place (Figure 7-13).

5 When you come to the bridge end, first set the bridge in place, supporting it with the two posts. The whole works must be linked with horizontal dowel rails running through the bottom holes. Contain the shaft with the two halves of the split ball, and then pivot the ball by means of two short lengths of dowel. This isn't easy because nothing has been glued together, but just do your best. Use a knife point to tease the dowel

FIGURE 7-15
If you have got it right, the top rail will hold the grub dowel in place so that it is contained between the shaft and the rail (see Figure 7-2A top right detail).

stubs through the bridge hole until they're well into the ball and clear of the top rail hole (Figure 7-14).

6 Take the two top rail dowels and run them through the bridge and into the post so the two components are linked and the stub dowels are contained (Figure 7-15).

7 When you are happy with the overall fit of the shaft in the ball, remove the shaft, and spend some time making sure the structure is square and stable, with all the posts and rails cut to length and tidy. If you have got it right, the whole works will be a good tight fit (Figure 7-16).

8 You will almost certainly have to make adjustments. For example, I found I needed to lengthen and ease the sliding section of the shaft at the handle end (Figure 7-17). You should be able to squeeze the halves of the ball together, with the shaft still a nice sliding fit.

9 Trim the coupling pins to length and hold them in place with the little dowel ring (Figure 7-18).

10 Sand all surfaces to a smooth finish, rub Danish oil on appropriate surfaces, glue the balls together so that the shafts are contained, and set the balls on their pivots.

11 Finally, give the whole works another sanding, rub on another thin coat of oil, and burnish all the surfaces with a thin application of beeswax.

PROBLEM SOLVING

■ While this project looks complicated, the only really tricky parts are fitting the cross coupling tubes and making sure the balls pivot properly. Use double-sided tape to hold the ball halves together during the trial assembly.

■ To my mind, the most clever aspect of this design is the way the dowel stubs are held in place. In fact, the various parts don't need to be glued. However, success comes from the stub dowels being just the right length and a smooth push fit.

■ Since the moving parts need to be smooth turning, it's a good idea to lightly wax and burnish mating faces: the slide shafts, inside the ball and inside the crossed coupling.

■ If you like the project except for the woodturning required, you could modify the design and use cubes instead of balls.

FIGURE 7-16
Trim the bridge to shape, and cut a short length of dowel for the decorative detail at top center.

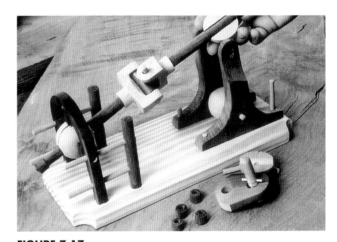

FIGURE 7-17
Try out various shaft angles and modify the length of the sliding necks accordingly.

FIGURE 7-18
Fit the little stop rings on the ends of the coupling pivots.

Camshaft Valve

PROJECT BACKGROUND

Apart from my wife Gill, my pride and joy is an old Land Rover four-wheel-drive vehicle. It's a diesel, made in 1975, with uncomfortable seats, ungodly noisy and painted military green—a wonderful machine! It ran like a gem for the first few weeks, and then started to smoke like a bonfire! I'll spare you the mechanic's lengthy explanation, but the problem was diagnosed as a sticking valve. So there we all were, up to our armpits in grease and tools, when Gill spotted something, suddenly reached into the air intake and pulled out a squirrel's tail. Nothing else, just a slightly charred tail! The good news is the problem is solved—no sticking valves, no more smoke, and no more squirrel! My sudden immersion in engine disassembly paid off also in terms of another wooden mechanism, this one honoring those hard-working valves.

PROJECT OVERVIEW

Study the project picture above, the working drawings (Figure 8-2A) and the template designs (Figure 8-2B). Note how this project shows the various elements of a valve-train as flat components mounted to a back board. In action, the crank handle is turned so that the cam on the back of the handle pushes up on the rod. The rod in turn pushes up the rocker arm, which pivots like a see-saw and pushes down the valve, opening it. This action is possible by the fact that the rocker arm is weighted with lead shot, so that while it's easy to lift, it nevertheless wants to fall back to the closed position.

The skill level for this project is low in terms of building the pieces, while the assembly aspect can be tricky, with a lot of finicky small parts that break easily. Once you have the cam in place and have added weight to the end of the rocker, then it all comes together easily.

PROJECT EIGHT: WORKING DRAWING

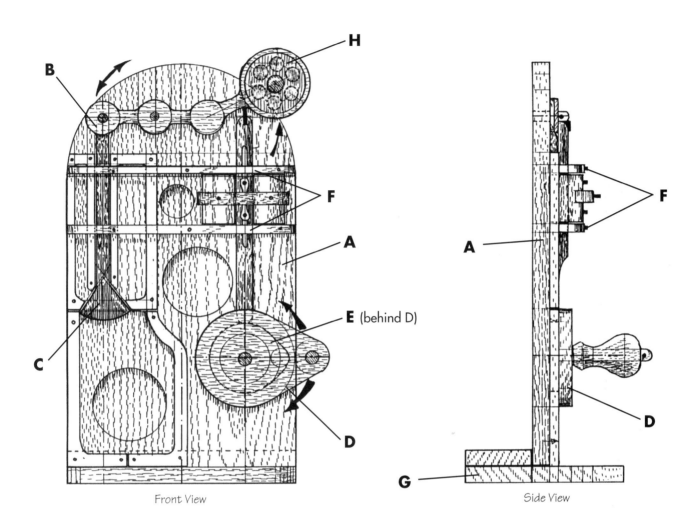

B

H

F

A

E (behind D)

C

D

Front View

A

F

D

G

Side View

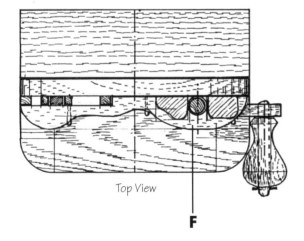

Top View

F

FIGURE 8-2A

Note how the weight is needed on the end of the rocker arm so that the arm is always falling down to make contact with the top of the push rod.

A *Back board*
B *Rocker arm*
C *Valve*
D *Crank handle*
E *Cam plate*
F *Rod and valve guide*
G *Base board*
H *Valve counterweight*

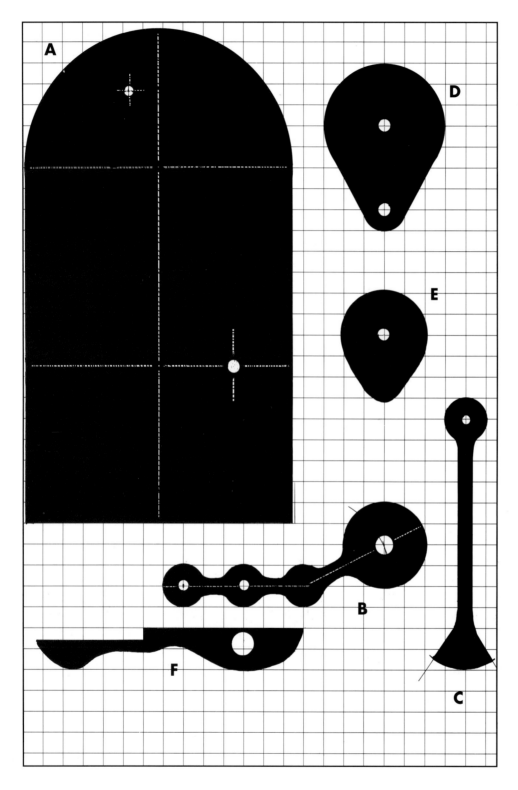

FIGURE 8-2B
The template design at a scale of two grid squares to 1 inch.
A *Back board*
B *Rocker arm*
C *Valve*
D *Crank handle*
E *Cam plate*
F *Rod and valve guide*

NOTE
As with any wooden sculpture, the dimensions indicated are starting points only. Modify dimensions, spacers and parts as necessary.

CUTTING LIST

Note: All measurements are in inches, and the sizes allow for a generous amount of waste. The small parts aren't listed, and the sizes given only allow for single components.

Part	Item	Dimensions T W L
A	Back board	¾ x 7 x 13
B	Rocker arm	⅝ x 4 x 8
C	Valve	½ x 2 x 7
D	Crank handle	½ x 4 x 5
E	Cam plate	⅜ x 2½ x 3
F	Rod and valve guide	⅜ x 1½ x 7
G	Base board	¾ x 5½ x 7
H	Valve counterweight	½ x 2½ x 2½

CHOOSING YOUR WOOD

You can use just about any wood you like. Just be sure it's free from splits and knots, is attractive to the eye, dry and relatively easy to work. We chose pine for the base and the back boards, larch for the cylinder chamber walls, mahogany for the crank, valve and rocker weight, shop-bought dowels for the push rod, and anything on hand for the bits and pieces.

MAKING THE BACK AND BASE BOARDS

1 Study the working drawing (Figure 8-2A), then plane the wood for these parts to a finished thickness of ½".

2 Square the wood edges with a square and plane. Draw out the design onto the wood. The 6¾" circle goes on the top of the back board, and the 1" radiuses on the front of the base board.

3 Mark the position of all the parts and the two pivot holes—the one for the rocker arm and the one for the crank handle.

4 Drill the holes with a bit that matches your dowels, then cut out the two boards on your scroll saw. Sand all the sawn edges to a smooth finish.

5 With a rule and square, double-check your measurements and component positions against the working drawing, especially the position of the two pivot holes.

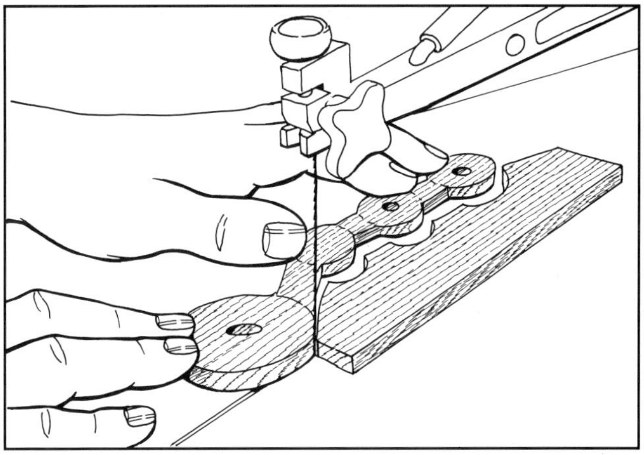

FIGURE 8-3

If you use a new fine-tooth blade and make sure that it's well tensioned, then you will find that the sawn edges hardly need to be sanded. Scroll saw blades are cheap enough, there's no need to use a blade until it's toothless.

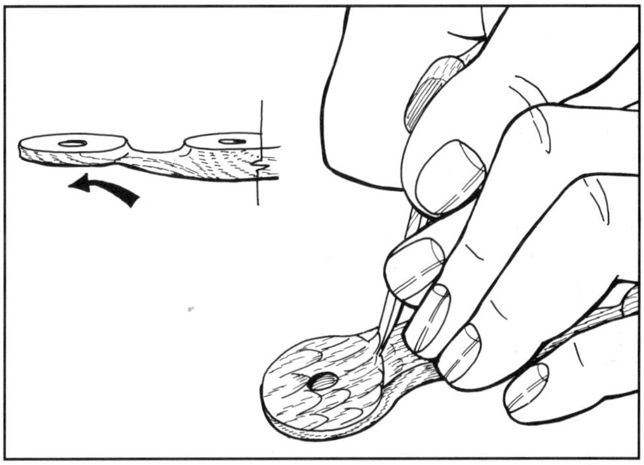

FIGURE 8-4

Slice away half the thickness of the wood around the area of the pivot.

MAKING THE ROCKER ARM

1 Plane your wood to a finished thickness of about ⅜". Then study the working drawings (Figure 8-2A), noting how the design of the rocker arm is based on four circles. Three of the circles are 1" diameter, while the fourth is 2⅛" diameter. Note also how the three small circles are set 1½" apart on the same center line.

2 Use rule, pencil and compass to draw out the design on the wood, then drill the holes with a bit sized to match your dowels. Cut out the profile on your scroll saw (Figure 8-3).

3 Use a pencil to label the best face, then take a knife or chisel and pare away half the thickness of the small valve-pivot circle. Make sure that you only cut away the back face (Figure 8-4).

4 Use a knife and sandpaper to work the neck area between the circles to a rounded shape. The original compass-drawn circles are left as flats (Figure 8-5).

MAKING THE VALVE

1 Plane the wood you chose for the valve down to a finished thickness of ¼".

2 Run a center line down the length of the grain, and mark two points 6" apart. Draw out the design on these two points so one is the rocker pivot and the other the intersection of the curve of the valve.

3 Lay out the valve design between these two points, with the stem about ½" wide, and the part-circle curve of the valve based on a 1⅜" radius.

4 Drill a hole through the pivot point that matches your dowel, then cut the shape out on your scroll saw. Before you cut, check that the distance between the pivot center and the bottom of the curve is 6" (see Figure 8-7).

5 Set the stem with the best face up against a suitable stop—a bench dog or shop-made bench hook—and use a chisel to pare the pivot circle down to about half its thickness (Figure 8-6).

6 Finally, do a trial assembly of the rocker and valve. If all is well, the two half-thickness pieces should fit together so from one piece to the other the faces are flush (Figure 8-7).

MAKING THE ROD AND VALVE GUIDES

1 Because the guides are difficult to make and fit, start by studying the working drawings (Figure 8-2A). Note the way that the guides are cut from thin wood, with the various elements within the forms guiding and containing both the valve and the push rod. You'll see how one end of the guide bridges the walls of the chamber to contain the stem of the valve, while the other end is drilled to take the stem of the push rod. Consider also how the guides are set parallel to each other, so that they contain the guide blocks that hold the little bridge-and-plate apparatus against the top face of the rod.

FIGURE 8-5
Use a knife and sandpaper to rub the necks down to a rounded finish. Note how the circles are left untouched.

FIGURE 8-6
Hold the chisel bevel down so that the blade is always trying to rise out of the wood.

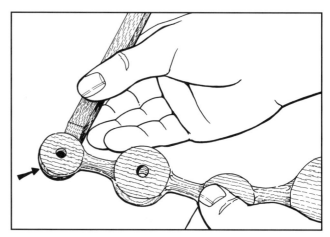

FIGURE 8-7
Try the two components together, and make adjustments so they add up to the total thickness and can pivot flush.

2 Plane the wood to a finished thickness of ¼", and draw the design out on one piece.

3 Sandwich the two pieces together so that the drawn design is uppermost. I used small tabs of double-sided tape to do this. Then treat the sandwiched pieces as a single unit, and drill the rod hole and cut out the profile.

4 Ease the sandwich apart, leaving you with two identical parts. Use a knife to trim the top edge to a rounded finish (Figure 8-8).

MAKING THE CHAMBER WALLS

1 Once again study the working drawings (Figure 8-2A), noting how the top middle section of the chamber acts as a guide for the stem of the valve, with the stem being contained by two walls and bridged by the guide. Note also how, apart from the two guide walls and the two gates at the bottom of the valve, the chamber walls themselves can be any shape that takes your fancy.

2 When you have decided what shape and size you want the walls to be, plane your wood down to a thickness of ¼". Trace the various designs from your working drawings, and press-transfer the traced lines through to the wood.

3 Be careful with the thin sections as they'll be very fragile across the short grain curves. Very carefully cut the walls out on your scroll saw (Figure 8-9).

ASSEMBLY AND FINISHING

1 Lay out all the parts and check them over for possible problems. Don't worry at this stage about final sanding as we're going to do a trial assembly first. Just make sure that the little cut-outs aren't going to let you down—you don't want any splits or loose knots to spoil the integrity of the structure.

2 Give all the components a quick sanding with fine grade sandpaper, then wipe them over with a small amount of Danish oil—just enough to seal the grain. Keep the oil away from areas that will be glued later.

3 Start by using a dowel to pin the rocker arm at the top of the board. Then take the push rod (see the detail drawings for how it was slotted and pared to a flat face, with a little piece of hardwood fitted at the top) and fit it in place with the little link-and-pin component.

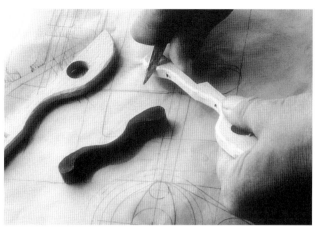

FIGURE 8-8
Use a knife to trim the top edge to a rounded profile—like a round nosing.

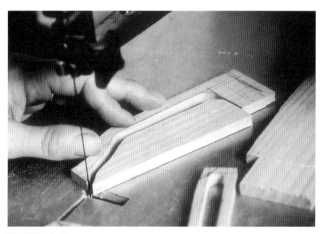

FIGURE 8-9
Be careful, when you are cutting across the run of the grain, that you don't split the resultant short grain.

FIGURE 8-10
See how the little link shape needs to sit level with the flat face. Note also how the bottom end of the rod is sliced down to about half the thickness so that it's the same thickness as the cam.

FIGURE 8-11
Add as much weight as possible. It's important that the weight pulls the end of the rocker arm down against the top of the push rod.

Note how the function of the link is twofold: it allows the rod to slide up and down, while at the same time holding the rod in place against the back board (Figure 8-10).

4 Take the disk that you made for the weighted end of the rocker and cut pieces of lead to fit into the drilled pockets (Figure 8-11, 8-12). Use either lead shot or fishing sinkers—you'll find both at most large sporting goods stores. Sand the disk smooth on the pocket side, because it needs to fit flush with the rocker.

5 Put the rocker arm, the weight disk and the short length of fixing dowel in place, and see how everything fits.

6 Slide the rocker in place so the bits of lead are contained (Figure 8-13). Unfortunately, the decorative detailing of the pockets is hidden as I designed it here, but you can experiment with ways to display it.

7 Fit the chamber walls in place with wooden pegs, and set the two guides across the width of the board so the valve is contained. It's important that the movement be easy. If anything sticks, then sand one or all the components until the action works properly.

8 Slide the push rod in place and again try out the movement (Figure 8-14).

9 Set the two little blocks in place between the horizontal guides at either side of the push rod. Then set the link down between the blocks so that the fixing sticks go down through the slot that runs up the middle of the push rod (Figure 8-15).

FIGURE 8-12
The more weight the merrier—if you can find a way of casting little disks to fill the holes, then so much the better.

FIGURE 8-13
Rub the mating faces down so that they fit flush together.

10 Set the cam on the crank pivot, then slide the crank arm in place (Figure 8-16). It's not easy to test the movement at this stage because the cam and the crank aren't yet glued together, but at least make sure that the crank is able to turn without bumping into the side of the push rod. If this is a problem, then lower the flat face at the bottom end of the rod until it's much lower than the underside of the crank.

FIGURE 8-14
Make adjustments so that the drilled guide holes, the push rod and the crank pivot are all perfectly aligned.

11 Put the handle on the crank, the little bridge in place across the push rod guide blocks, and do another dry run.

12 When you're happy with the movement, disassemble the whole works, sand all the surfaces and edges smooth, apply Danish oil again, and glue things up. When dry, give everything a light sanding, then burnish with beeswax.

PROBLEM SOLVING

■ This is one of those projects that needs to be continually tested for fit as the various parts are made. Find a way to temporarily tack parts together, such as using bits of Blue Tack, small strips of double-sided tape or tiny drops of Super Glue. The Super Glue gives the best hold, but you must be absolutely sure to only use tiny amounts—no more than a pinpoint.

■ If you want to use the weighted disk but also want to have some part of the pockets showing as a decorative feature, here's a solution. Make the drilled pockets so they're a stepped hole that will trap steel ball bearings. This way the ball bearings will show through the holes on the face of the weight disk but still be held in place.

■ To get a more elegant look, use better woods such as plum, lime and boxwood. The texture of these woods gives a fine finish and beautiful colors.

FIGURE 8-15
Note how the two blocks both nicely distance the guides and contain the push rod.

FIGURE 8-16
See how the bottom end of the push rod has been shaved down to the thickness of the cam so that it doesn't get in the way of the crank.

Water Lift Pump

PROJECT BACKGROUND

When we were first married, Gill and I lived in a farm cottage that had a well and a pump to draw our water. I was forever climbing down into the well to sort out the leather flap valve at the bottom of the pump chamber. It would get blocked with mud, stones, grit, dead frogs and all manner of things. Life with such rustic charm was never lacking in wet, muddy, cold chores.

That old lift pump was a beautifully simple piece of machinery. Basically it's just two valves working together. When the handle is lifted, the rod goes down, the valve at the bottom of the chamber closes, the valve at the bottom of the piston opens and water rushes to the top side of the piston. When the pump handle is pushed down, the rod comes up, the valve at the bottom of the chamber opens, the valve in the piston closes and water floods the bottom chamber, ready for the next pump stroke.

PROJECT OVERVIEW

Study the project picture at left, the working drawings (Figure 9-2A) and the template designs (Figure 9-2B). While the various components are relatively easy to make, the assembly is convoluted. The problem is the component parts are short grained and fragile, with lots of curved slender sections that run across the grain, plus there are lots of parts. The measurements can be modified, except for the rod and chamber lengths. If you want to alter the size of the project, use stiff paper and pins to build a prototype first.

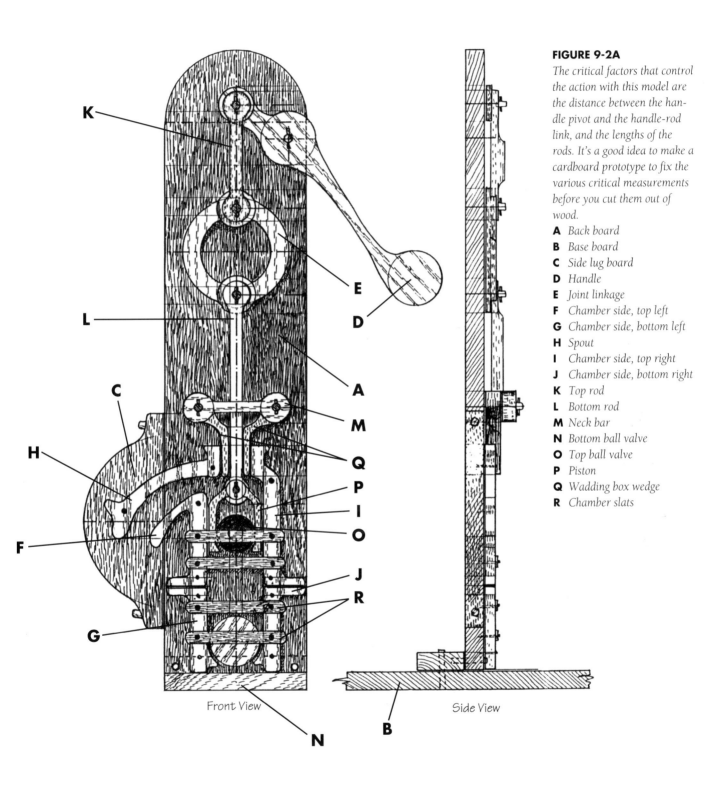

FIGURE 9-2A

The critical factors that control the action with this model are the distance between the handle pivot and the handle-rod link, and the lengths of the rods. It's a good idea to make a cardboard prototype to fix the various critical measurements before you cut them out of wood.

A *Back board*
B *Base board*
C *Side lug board*
D *Handle*
E *Joint linkage*
F *Chamber side, top left*
G *Chamber side, bottom left*
H *Spout*
I *Chamber side, top right*
J *Chamber side, bottom right*
K *Top rod*
L *Bottom rod*
M *Neck bar*
N *Bottom ball valve*
O *Top ball valve*
P *Piston*
Q *Wadding box wedge*
R *Chamber slats*

Front View

Side View

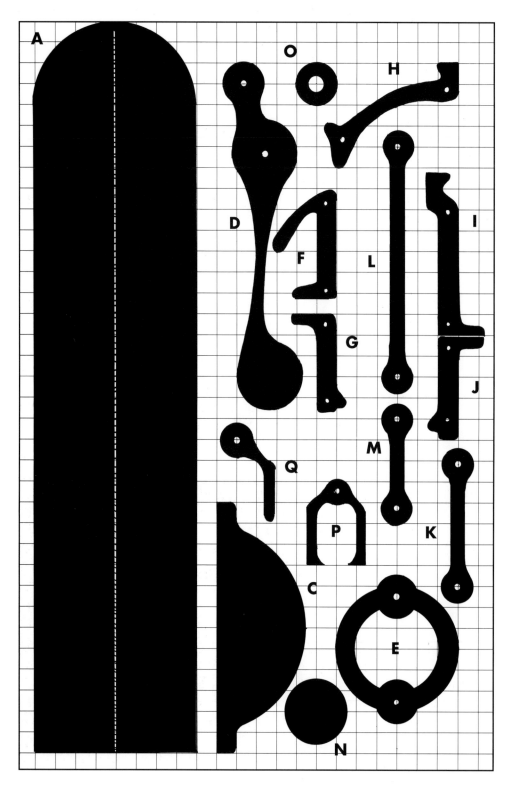

FIGURE 9-2B

The template design at a scale of two grid squares to 1 inch. Note that we have only illustrated the difficult-to-visualize components.

A *Back board*
B *Base board*
C *Side lug board*
D *Handle*
E *Joint linkage*
F *Chamber side, top left*
G *Chamber side, bottom left*
H *Spout*
I *Chamber side, top right*
J *Chamber side, bottom right*
K *Top rod*
L *Bottom rod*
M *Neck bar*
N *Bottom ball valve*
O *Top ball valve*
P *Piston*
Q *Wadding box wedge*
R *Chamber slats*

NOTE

As with any wooden sculpture, the dimensions indicated are starting points only. Modify dimensions, spacers and parts as necessary.

CUTTING LIST

Note: All measurements are in inches, and the sizes allow for a generous amount of waste.

Part	Item	Dimensions T W L
A	Back board	¾ x 4½ x 18
B	Base board	¾ x 4½ x 12
C	Side lug board	¾ x 3 x 6½
D	Handle	½ x 2½ x 9
E	Joint linkage	½ x 4 x 4
F	Chamber side, top left	½ x 2 x 3
G	Chamber side, bottom left	½ x 2 x 3
H	Spout	½ x 2 x 4½
I	Chamber side, top right	½ x 2 x 4½
J	Chamber side, btm right	½ x 2 x 3
K	Top rod	½ x 1 x 4½
L	Bottom rod	½ x 1 x 7
M	Neck bar	½ x 1 x 3½
N	Bottom ball valve	½ x 2 x 2
O	Top ball valve	½ x 1½ x 1½
P	Piston	½ x 2 x 3
Q	Wadding box wedge	½ x 2 x 3
R	Chamber slats	¹⁄₁₆ x ⅜ x 3

CHOOSING YOUR WOOD

You can use just about any wood you like, just make sure it's dry, easy to cut on a scroll saw and free of splits and knots. We used English brown oak for the base and back boards, American oak for the handle and scrap pieces of pine, cherry and plum for the rest. Select woods that have rich color and grain patterns from one component to the next.

MAKING THE BACK, BASE AND LUG BOARDS

1 Study the design (Figures 9-2A&B), noting how the base board, back board and the small lug board are made from ½"-thick wood, with the various curves drawn with a compass. The greater part of the base is set to the front of the back board, with the two boards fixed by a glued-and-pegged batten.

2 Plane your wood to a finished thickness of ½". It should be free of splits and knots. If you're using a tough wood like the brown oak I used, then it's also a good idea to sight along its length checking for twists.

3 Draw the design out with a rule, square and compass, and cut the pieces out on your scroll saw.

4 Set the back board at right angles to the base and support it with a piece of scrap.

5 Decide where the lug needs to be positioned, and then dry fit it in place with a couple of dowels.

MAKING THE CHAMBER WALLS AND VALVE BALL

1 Plane the wood to a finished thickness of about ⁵⁄₁₆". Don't worry if it's a little oversize, as it's better to be slightly too thick than too thin, as long as the thickness is uniform.

2 Trace the design from the working drawings, then pencil press transfer the traced lines through to the best face of your wood. Remember to position the tracings so the grain runs up through the walls of the chamber.

3 With the design laid out, cut out the pieces on your scroll saw (Figure 9-3). While it's all pretty straightforward, be careful when you come to the curves. You don't want to go too fast or too hard and split the wood across the fragile short grain.

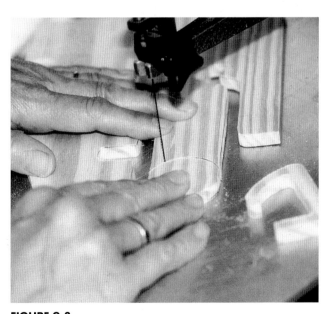

FIGURE 9-3
Work with a new, properly tensioned blade. Make sure you cut slightly to the waste side of the drawn line.

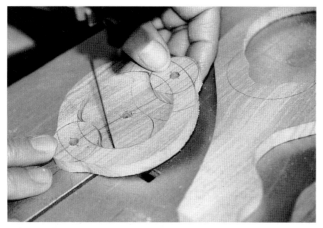

FIGURE 9-4

Note the little radius curves at the intersection of the drawn circles. These help to create the engineered and worked-in-steel look.

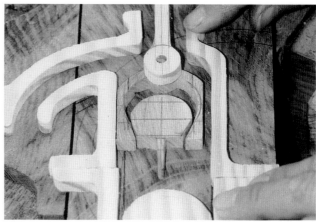

FIGURE 9-5

It's important that the side walls of the chamber are parallel to each other so the components within the chamber are free to move up and down.

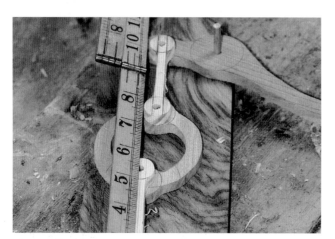

FIGURE 9-6

Check and double-check the measurements to ensure accuracy. If you made a mistake, then the easiest fix is to make a new top rod.

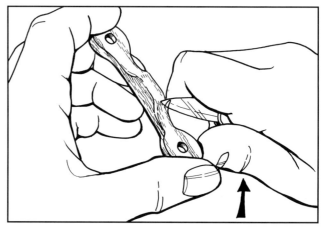

FIGURE 9-7

Work with a tight apple-paring stroke, with the thumb of the right hand controlling the length of the stroke. Always work with the run of the grain, from center to end—never the other way around!

MAKING THE LINKAGE

1 Study Figure 9-2A, noting how the linkage design is based on four circles. Two circles make up the basic hoop disk, and two smaller circles for the pivot linkage points.

2 Plane the wood to a finished thickness of about ⅜".

3 Draw a center line that runs the direction of the grain. Mark a point midway along the line, and draw out two circles one within the other. One should have a radius of 1" and the other a radius of 1½". Mark the center line halfway across the width of the hoop at top and bottom, then use a compass to draw two circles with a radius of ½".

4 Draw little radiuses at the intersections of all of the circles.

5 Drill the pivot points with a bit that matches your dowels. Then drill another hole through the waste area, and cut out the parts (Figure 9-4).

6 Make the handle and the piston.

MAKING THE RODS

1 Plane the wood to size, and use a rule, square and compass to draw out the design of the two rods. Have them about ⁵⁄₁₆" wide along their length, with ends based on ¾" diameter circles.

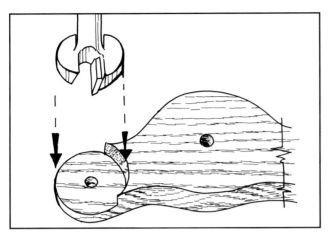

FIGURE 9-8
Note how a large diameter Forstner bit has been used to halve the thickness of the hand-rod pivot point.

2 Cut out the rods on your scroll saw, drill holes through the pivot centers, then check the fit of everything (Figure 9-5).

3 When you have fitted the two rods, the sum total length between the pivot point on the top end of the top rod and the pivot point on the bottom end of the bottom rod should be such that the piston fits on both the up and down strokes (Figure 9-6).

4 Once satisfied with the shape and size of the rods, use a knife to whittle the ends down to about half their thicknesses so the face of the pivot circle is smooth and flush. Work with a tight paring stroke from center to end, creating a nice, clean curve from the top face down (Figure 9-7).

5 Use a knife and fine sandpaper to give the rods and all other components a smooth finish.

ASSEMBLY AND FINISHING

1 Check over the parts for splits or warps (Figure 9-9). Make sure the various mating surfaces are to size so the parts can work together smoothly.

2 Do a trial assembly. Start by pegging the chamber sides and the wadding wedges onto the back board (Figure 9-10). Note how the wadding pins need to be long enough to take the neck bar.

3 Set the rods and the joint linkage in place with the pivot dowels a tight fit in the linkage and a loose fit through the rods (Figure 9-11). The bottom rod should be a nice snug fit between the wedges.

FIGURE 9-9
Check the components for problems. Be very careful when handling the chamber wall strips, as they're very fragile.

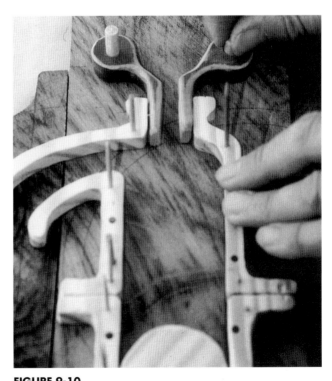

FIGURE 9-10
Note how the wishbone shape of the wadding box wedges helps to create a dynamic effect by directing the eye down and towards the chamber.

4 Set the large disk valve in place in the chamber, the piston on the bottom end of the rod and the neck bar in place across the wadding wedges. Sand any parts that are binding until you have a good fit (Figure 9-12).

5 Fit the valve in the piston and the slats across the chamber, then stand the whole works upright and test the movement (Figure 9-13).

6 When you have a smooth movement, and have determined what needs to be glued and pinned, disassemble and do a final finish sanding. Apply Danish oil to all surfaces except those faces being glued. Glue up, fit the small pins, and once dry, give the whole works a coat of beeswax.

PROBLEM SOLVING

■ With a complex project like this, you're continually fitting and modifying parts. This being so, save yourself some effort and hold off on fine sanding until the very end, after everything is working properly.

■ If the movement is stiff or crooked, then it could be that the handle pivot is badly placed on the back board. If so, drill a selection of holes and test each one for the best fit.

■ If you find the chamber slats less than beautiful, and you don't mind using a non-wood option, then cover the chamber with a clear Plexiglas plate.

FIGURE 9-11
The linkage pivot dowels need to be a tight fit in the linkage circle and a loose fit in the rod. At a later stage, you will have to hold the rod and various other components in place by running a thin wood pin through the dowel.

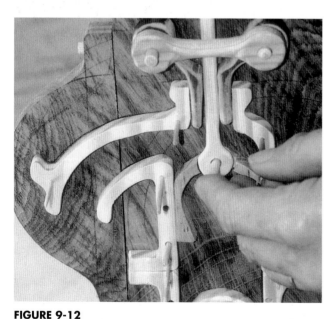

FIGURE 9-12
The piston is extremely fragile, and you might need to laminate it up from veneers to give it extra strength.

FIGURE 9-13
Note how the greater length of the base needs to be at the front so the machine is stable and won't tip forwards.

Lever & Ratchet Mechanism

PROJECT BACKGROUND

When we were first married, Gill and I lived in a cottage deep in the country, with no electricity and no indoor plumbing. We got by with lots of oil lamps and a well in the garden. We could've purchased a generator to provide power, but we were trying our very best to be self-sufficient. The most pressing problem was always how to lift the water up from the well to the storage tank on the roof. We tried hand pumps large and small, a foot pump, a wind-powered pump with propeller blades among other things, but none of them worked that well. The hand pumping was such hard work that I think I drank more water than I ever pumped up to the tank. Well, finally a local farmer took pity on me and showed me how to pump water up by means of a simple lever

and ratchet mechanism. Summarized, you lash one end of a rope to the top branches of a tall tree and the other to the mechanism. When the wind blows, the tree sways backward and forward, the rope repeatedly snatches at the lever, the ratchet inches round and a lift pump is set into motion. While doing it this way only brings up a teacup of water at each jerk of the lever, the wind was free and did all the work. Over time, the tank would fill bit by bit, and we didn't have to spend hours each day manning the hand pump. This is not the project for you if your goal is to impress your friends with dramatic action and movement. Instead, it's a wooden representation of one of those behind-the-scenes devices that makes our lives easier by quietly going about its business.

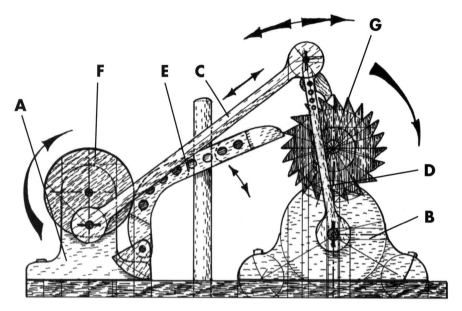

Front View

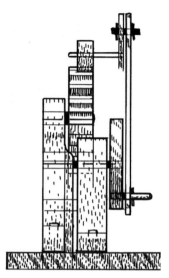

Side View

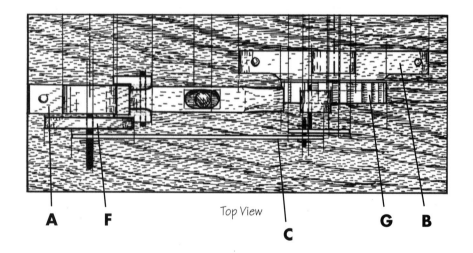

Top View

FIGURE 10-2A

With this project, note how the drive wheel needs to be turned in a clockwise direction.

A *Drive wheel stanchion*
B *Toothed wheel stanchion*
C *Long crank drive rod*
D *Short crank rod*
E *Control arm*
F *Drive wheel*
G *Toothed wheel*

PROJECT TEN: TEMPLATE DESIGN

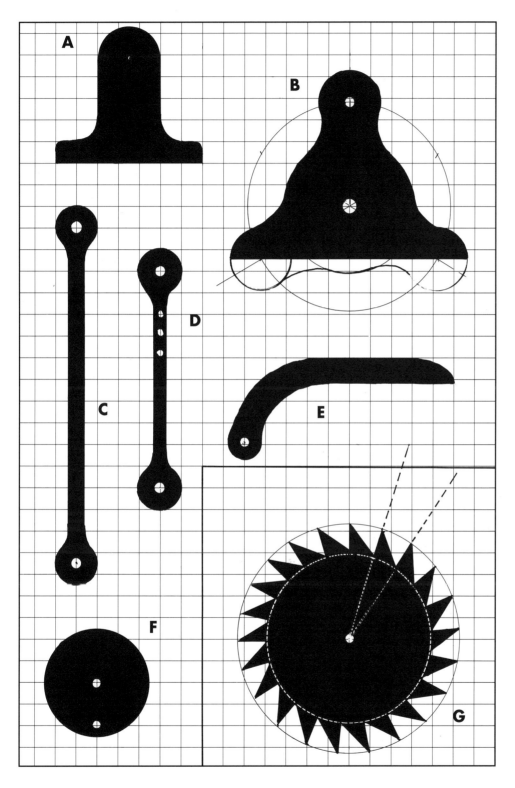

FIGURE 10-2B

The template design drawn to a scale of two grid squares to 1 inch (top), and four grid squares to 1 inch (bottom right). Note how the main stanchion is drawn out by means of a compass, with the radius curves between the circles being drawn by hand. Note also how the toothed wheel is drawn out.

A *Drive wheel stanchion*
B *Toothed wheel stanchion*
C *Long crank drive rod*
D *Short crank rod*
E *Control arm*
F *Drive wheel*
G *Toothed wheel*

NOTE

As with any wooden sculpture, the dimensions indicated are starting points only. Modify dimensions, spacers and parts as necessary.

CUTTING LIST

Note: All measurements are in inches, and the sizes listed allow for a generous amount of cutting waste. You might want to start out sizing things closer to finished dimensions. You can also save yourself some planing by choosing wood of the proper thickness. Note that we've only illustrated the critical or difficult-to-visualize components.

Part	Item	Dimensions T W L
A	Drive wheel stanchion	1 x 4 x 3½
B	Toothed wheel stanchion	1 x 6 x 5
C	Long crank drive rod	3⁄16 x 1¼ x 9½
D	Short crank rod	3⁄16 x 1¼ x 6
E	Control arm	1 x 3 x 7
F	Drive wheel	½ x 3 x 3
G	Toothed wheel	¾ x 4½ x 4½

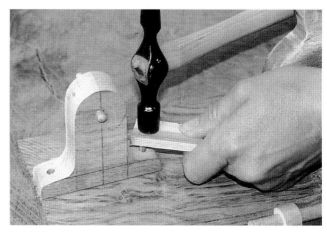

FIGURE 10-3
Use a small hammer and a block to drive the dowels home.

FIGURE 10-4
Butt the workpiece hard up against a stop (I'm using a bench hook), and use a gouge to skim the waste down to a depth of about ¼". Be careful that you don't run the gouge into end grain.

PROJECT OVERVIEW

Study the project photo, the working drawing (Figure 10-2A) and the template design (Figure 10-2B). Note that all the components are fixed to the base board, with the primary moving parts pivoting on stanchions. In action, the drive wheel is turned, the long crank rod goes forward, the little finger-drag component nudges and drags, and the toothed wheel goes around. The control arm ensures that the toothed wheel only turns in the one direction.

While the individual procedures are pretty straightforward, involving just some scroll saw work, drilling and whittling, assembling the machine is tricky. Or, if you're the optimistic sort, look at the assembly as a glorious challenge.

CHOOSING YOUR WOOD

The wonderful news is that you can use just about any wood—lime, oak, pine, beech, sycamore, maple, cherry, just about anything you find in your scrap bin. Just be sure the toothed wheel is made from a close-grained dense wood that's strong across short grain. And remember also that you're building something that a lot of people are going to want to try out, so choose wood that will hold up to a bit of rough usage.

MAKING THE STANCHIONS

1 Study the working drawings (Figure 10-2A) and the template designs (Figure 10-2B), so that you have a good understanding of how the project needs to be made and put together.

2 Take the wood that you have chosen for the base board and plane and cut it to size—it needs to be about ½" thick, 5" wide and 12" long.

3 Take the 1"-thick wood for the stanchions and plane it to a finished thickness of about ⅞". Draw the two images out to size, and fret them out on the scroll saw.

4 Take the drive wheel stanchion, run the holes through—for the main pivot and the fixing dowels—and then position it on the base and fix with dry dowels (Figure 10-3). It's important that the stanchion is fair and square with the base, so spend time getting it right.

FIGURE 10-5
Sand the form so that the raised circle runs in a smooth curve down to the level of the lowered waste.

5 Take the blank for the other stanchion, and use a compass set to a radius of 1½" to draw in the decorative casting circle.

6 Run the four holes through with the drill—two for pivots and two for fixing.

7 Take a small shallow-curve gouge; set the workpiece flat down on its back so that it is butted hard up against a stop with the front face uppermost. Then set to work cutting back the waste. Lower the waste little by little, with a series of shallow skimming cuts (Figure 10-4) until the casting circle is left standing proud by about ¼". If you have got it right, the two side lugs and the top head will finish up at about ⅜" thick.

8 When you are happy with the overall shape of the casting feature, use graded sandpapers to rub the contours down to a good finish. Work from rough through to smooth, with the sandpapers wrapped around a length of dowel (Figure 10-5).

MAKING THE CRANK RODS

1 Have a look at the working drawings and template designs (Figures 10-2A&B). The two crank rods are more or less the same shape—the same diameter ends and similar curves. The only real difference is that the long rod is ⅜" wide and the small rod ¼". Both rods are about ³⁄₁₆" thick.

2 Choose your wood with care. It doesn't matter too much if the grain is a bit wild, as long as overall it is sound and running along the length of the rod (Figure 10-6). To draw out the outer rods, start by

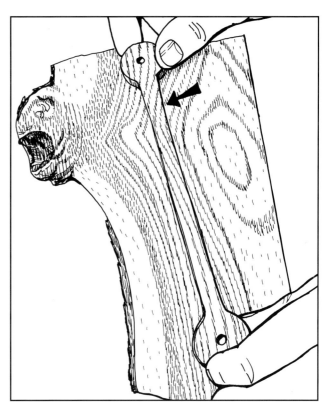

FIGURE 10-6
You always need to consider the run of the grain, especially if the component parts are long and slender. All that said, I'm not entirely happy with the grain on the right-hand end of the rod—it looks a little short grained and weak.

fixing the position of the end-centers. Draw a center line, measure the end-centers on the line, and use the compass to draw the end circles. Draw parallel lines each side of the center line; draw the radius curves freehand. Drill the pivot holes, and then finally fret out the total profile.

3 Fret out the drawn profiles on the scroll saw, and trim them up with a small knife so that all the angles are slightly rounded. They should look as if they might have been cast (Figure 10-7).

4 Finally, take the long rod and drill a line of four little holes at one end to give you fine-tuning choice when you come to the putting-together stage.

MAKING THE CONTROL ARM

1 Have a look at the working drawings (Figure 10-2A), and see how the function of the arm is to sit heavily on the toothed wheel so that the back-dragging action of the finger-drag component can't pull the wheel in reverse. Note how the arm is pivoted between two plates that are fixed at either side of the stanchion

FIGURE 10-7
Cut from end to middle so that you avoid running the blade into the end grain on the edge of the disk end.

FIGURE 10-8
Whittle the end of the arm so that it fits neatly between the pivot plates.

feet, with the width of the arm being reduced so that it fits between the plates. See also how the arm is held in alignment by being threaded on a large dowel post that is socketed into the base slab, with the threading hole being shaped so as to allow for movement.

2 When you have a clear picture of the shape and function of the arm, draw the image out on your chosen wood and fret it out on the scroll saw.

3 Run the holes through to match the diameter of your chosen dowels, and then use a knife to shape up the details—the narrowing at the tip and the pivot area, and the free shape around the large posthole (Figure 10-8).

MAKING THE TOOTHED WHEEL

1 Use a compass to draw two circles, one within the other—the outer with a radius of 1½", and the inner with a radius of about 1¼". Use a pair of dividers to run 22 equal step-offs around the circumference of the large circle. You could use math and a protractor to set the size of the step-offs (360° divided by 22

= 16.36°), but it's so much easier to go for a guesstimate size and to work the step-offs out by trial and error. Draw radius lines from the resultant intersections. Lastly, draw diagonals across each of the step-offs.

2 With all the guidelines in place, use a band or scroll saw and slowly cut out the teeth (Figure 10-9).

PUTTING TOGETHER AND FINISHING

1 Now comes the finger-aching task of having a dry run put together. Don't worry about fine sanding at this stage, just make sure that everything is tickerty-boo and all present and correct (Figure 10-10)—no splits or warping. When you are satisfied that all is correct, wipe the surfaces (barring those that are going to be glued) with a small amount of oil.

2 Set the two stanchions in place on the base and fix them with stubs of dowel.

3 Fit the control arm post, slide the main pivots in place in the stanchions, and fit the drive wheel (Figure 10-11).

FIGURE 10-9

Don't be tempted to rush this task. The teeth need to be cut with care, and, more than that, the band saw is potentially a very dangerous machine.

FIGURE 10-10

Give all the component parts a swift rub down—just enough to remove the worst of the sawn edges—and then give them their first wipe over with oil.

4 Take the control arm, pivot it between the little plates (Figure 10-12), and then fix it in position at the bottom of the drive wheel stanchion.

5 With the control arm in place and located on the alignment post, slide the toothed wheel on its pivot, and make fine adjustments—to the pointed end of the arm and/or the size of the alignment post hole (Figure 10-13).

6 Pivot the little finger-drag block in place in one or other of the four holes (Figure 10-14). Note that you might well need to drill another hole—it all depends on the shape of your finger-drag and the shape of the teeth on your wheel.

7 Fit the short crank rod in place, set the finger-drag in position, and then link the drive wheel and the top of the short crank with the long crank. The long dowel at bottom right gets cut back later (Figure 10-15).

FIGURE 10-11

Fit the large diameter dowel rod in the center of the stanchion. Note the spacer that is used to distance the crank so that it doesn't wander from side to side.

FIGURE 10-12

I built each pivot plate up in two layers so that the two plates could be stepped at either side of the stanchion.

FIGURE 10-13

Fiddle around with the length of the arm and the shape of the post-hole until the pointed end of the arm comes nicely to rest on the toothed wheel.

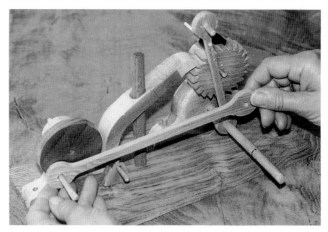

FIGURE 10-15

If the length of the rod is such that the finger-drag unit fails to do its stuff, then consider fitting the drag in the next hole down.

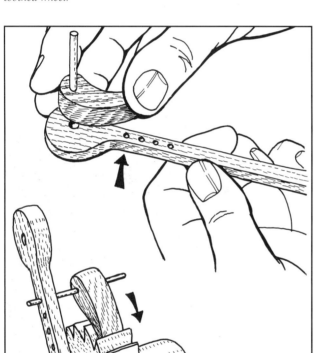

FIGURE 10-14

Locate the little pivot in one of the four holes in the shaft of the rod, as indicated by the top black arrow above.

8 When you have struggled to get all the parts in place, then have a trial turn and see if the finger-drag does its thing (Figure 10-16). Be mindful that you might have to make adjustments to one or all of the moving parts.

9 When you have achieved what you consider to be a good movement, then disassemble, and rub all the parts down to a fine finish.

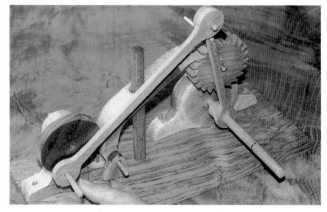

FIGURE 10-16

When you have got the movement right, then you can cut the various dowels to length and fit the holding pins.

10 Finally, glue up, rub the whole works down with oil, let the oil dry, and wax polish. Then the machine is finished and ready for showing.

PROBLEM SOLVING

■ If you look closely at Figure 10-15, you will see that there is a drilled hole on the top end of the short crank rod, just to the left of the pivot. This is a mistake—an aberration that occurred when I was trying to figure out how to fit the finger-drag component.

■ If the side-to-side movements of the two crank rods are a bit slack and messy, then you might well consider sandwiching the long rod between a couple of posts.

■ If you decide to use a band saw to cut the toothed wheel, then you must for safety's sake control the workpiece with a couple of push sticks—it's too small to be handheld.

Screw Jack

PROJECT BACKGROUND

The screw jack is a mechanism in common use for raising heavy weights through short lifts. It consists of a powerful combination of teeth and pinions enclosed in a metal frame, stock or box. If you are interested in math and have got a year or two to spend reading up, then there is a whole mountain of figures on the screw jack: the ratio between the number of teeth, the diameter of the wheel, the length of the handle, and so on. All you really need to know is that if a man or woman is able to raise about 50 pounds in weight, then they will, by means of a jack, be able to raise about twenty times this weight (about 5 tons). The jack is usually fitted out with a simple mechanism known as a pall and/or ratchet that stops the motion when it begins to run back.

PROJECT OVERVIEW

The jack is made up of three primary parts: the small gear wheel, the large gear wheel, and the long toothed bar or rack—all pegged and pivoted on a frame. The toothed and slotted rack is held in place by means of a long plate, with the two dowels that run through the plate also controlling the height of the movement. The little pall mechanism that sits just above the large wheel is pegged into a slot in such a way that it rises, falls and jams the mechanism so that the rack is held in place. When you want to bring the rack down, you simply raise the pall, flip it over and then wind back. The success of the project has to do with cutting the teeth. If you like working with rule and compass, and if you have a scroll saw, then you are going to get a good deal of pleasure from this project.

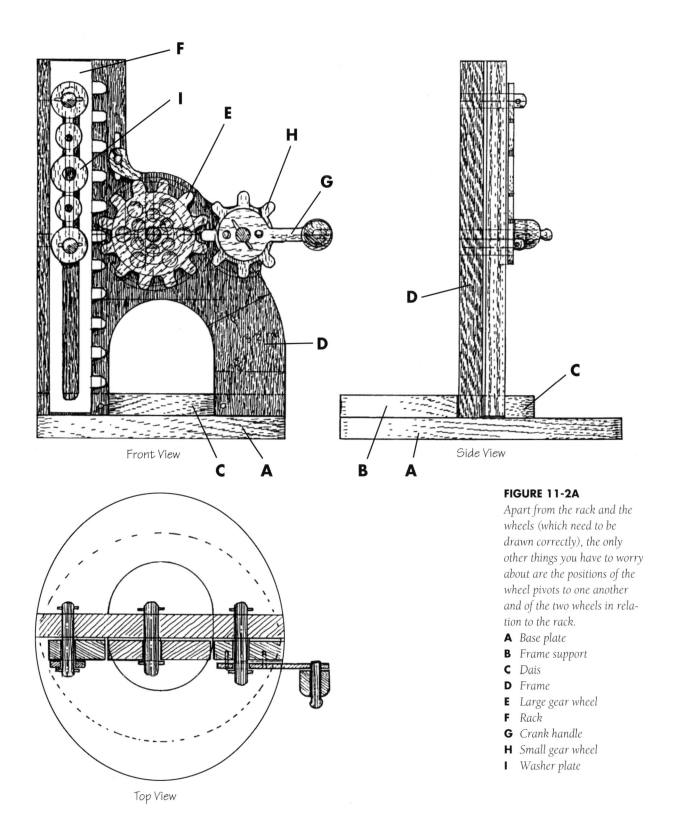

Front View

Side View

Top View

FIGURE 11-2A

Apart from the rack and the wheels (which need to be drawn correctly), the only other things you have to worry about are the positions of the wheel pivots to one another and of the two wheels in relation to the rack.

A *Base plate*
B *Frame support*
C *Dais*
D *Frame*
E *Large gear wheel*
F *Rack*
G *Crank handle*
H *Small gear wheel*
I *Washer plate*

PROJECT ELEVEN: TEMPLATE DESIGN

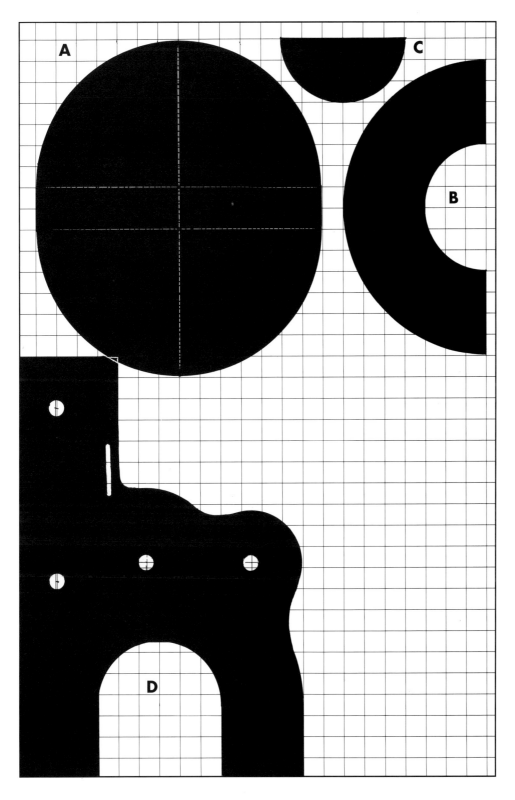

FIGURE 11-2B
The template design at a scale of two grid squares to 1 inch.
A Base plate
B Frame support
C Dais
D Frame

NOTE
As with any wooden sculpture, the dimensions indicated are starting points only. Modify dimensions, spacers and parts as necessary.

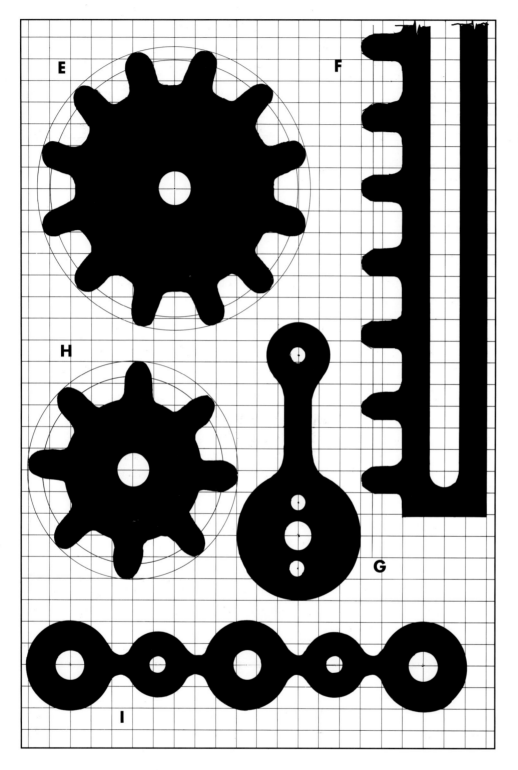

FIGURE 11-2C
The template design at a scale of four grid squares to 1 inch.
E *Large gear wheel*
F *Rack*
G *Crank handle*
H *Small gear wheel*
I *Washer plate*

NOTE
As with any wooden sculpture, the dimensions indicated are starting points only. Modify dimensions, spacers and parts as necessary.

CUTTING LIST		
Note: All measurements are in inches, and the sizes allow for a generous amount of waste.		
Part	Item	Dimensions T W L
A	Base plate	¾ x 8 x 9
B	Frame support	¾ x 8 x 8
C	Dais	Cut from frame support
D	Frame	¾ x 8 x 12
E	Large gear wheel	¼ x 3½ x 3½
F	Rack	¾ x 2½ x 12
G	Crank handle	¼ x 2 x 3½
H	Small gear wheel	¾ x 3 x 3
I	Washer plate	½ x 1¼ x 6

CHOOSING YOUR WOOD

This is one of those projects where you need to be pretty choosy over your wood. I say this, because the success of the project hinges on the teeth being cut and worked with care—with all the teeth being nicely shaped. And of course, it's no good working with a loose-grained easy-to-cut wood that is likely to split and/or crumble. If a tooth splits off, then the project is ruined. What all this amounts to, is that the wood needs to be hard and dense grained, so that it leaves the saw with the edges being hard and well defined. I used salvaged mahogany for the frame and the large wheel, cherry for the small wheel, straight-grained pine for the rack, oak for the base, and bits and bobs for all the rest. If you are short of wood, then best save the choice bits for the toothed components—meaning the two wheels and the rack.

MAKING THE FRAME AND BASE

1 When you have spent a good long time studying the working drawings and designs—so that you have a clear picture in your mind as to what goes where and how—take the wood that you have chosen for the frame and the base, and plane it down to a finished thickness of about ⅝". Not to worry if it's a wee bit thicker, as long as it's a uniform thickness overall.

2 Notice how the frame and the base plate are in the main achieved by using a compass, and the little dais piece is no more or less than the waste cut from the frame support. This done, then use the rule, square and compass to set the lines of the design out on the best face of the wood.

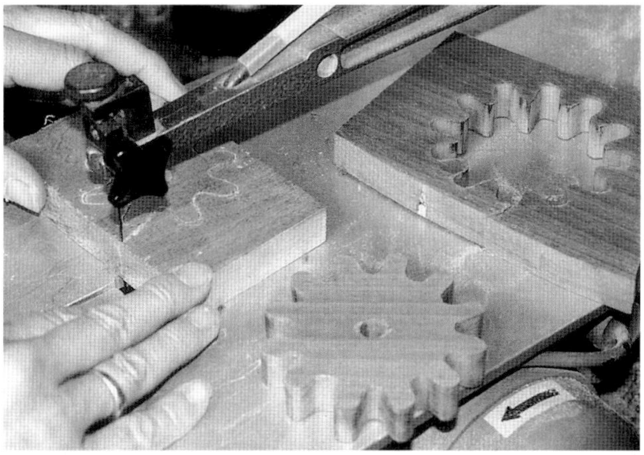

FIGURE 11-3

Take extra care when you are fretting out the wheels. Keep the line of cut slightly to the waste side of the drawn line, and make sure that the saw table is correctly set—meaning at right angles to the run of the blade.

3 Fret the profile out on the scroll saw.

4 Establish the precise position of the various pivot holes, then run them through with a bit size to match up with the diameter of your chosen dowels.

MAKING THE GEAR WHEELS AND THE RACK

1 Plane your wood to a finished thickness of about ½" for both wheels and the rack.

2 Use a compass to draw the two circles out on the wood—the large one with a radius of 1⅝", the small one with a radius of 1¼".

3 Trace the designs from your working drawings, and then transfer the traced imagery to the best face of the wood. Use the circles as an alignment guide.

4 Run the three components through with drilled holes—at the center of the two wheels and at each end of the rack slot.

5 Fit a new fine-toothed blade in the scroll saw, adjust the tension, and make sure that the saw table is at a right angle to the blade.

6 Finally, fret out the design. Take your time and go slowly so that all the sawn faces are crisp and smooth (Figure 11-3).

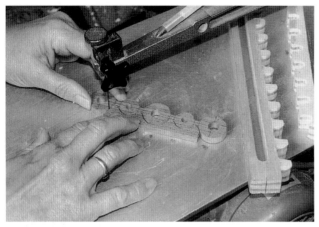

FIGURE 11-4
Do your best to ensure that the sawn lines are smooth-running and nicely curved. If the saw feels to be hard going, then wax the table to cut down on friction, and check that the blade is in good condition and well tensioned.

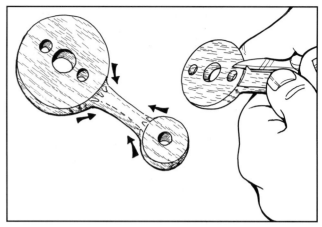

FIGURE 11-5
Whittle the arm to a rounded finish so that a little curve runs down from the flat face of the circle. Work from ends through to center.

MAKING THE WASHER PLATE AND THE CRANK HANDLE

1 Plane your chosen wood down to a thickness between ³⁄₁₆" and ¼".

2 Draw the imagery out on the best face of the wood, run the holes through with the appropriate size bits, and then fret the profiles out on the scroll saw. Go at it very slowly, all the while doing your very best to ensure that the line of cut is crisp and smooth—no stop-start steps or ragged cuts (Figure 11-4).

3 When you have achieved the cut-out for the crank handle, first drill the two peg-fixing holes—through the crank and the small wheel—and then take a small knife and trim the arm to a rounded finish (Figure 11-5).

PUTTING TOGETHER AND FINISHING

1 When you have achieved all the component parts that go to make up the project, set them out best face uppermost, and systematically check them over for potential problems (Figure 11-6). Okay, so I always say this, but the sad fact is that projects of this type and character are often less than beautiful, or are that much less successful, simply because such and such a part is flawed or needs to be re-cut.

2 Don't worry at this trial run stage about a fine finish; just make sure that the edges are free from splinters and jags.

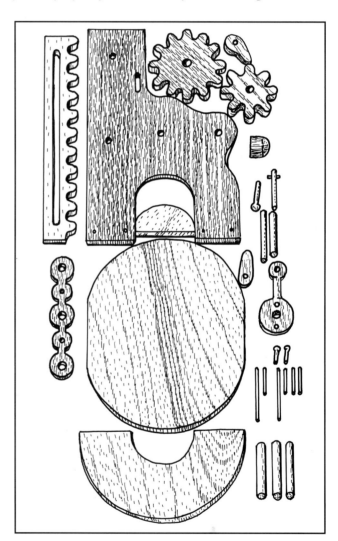

FIGURE 11-6
Check the components to make sure that they are free from splits, and then give them a swift rub down in readiness for the dry trial run putting together.

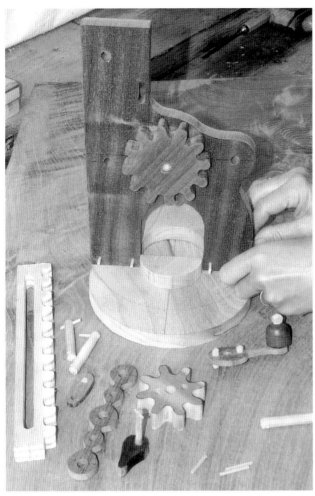

FIGURE 11-7
Set the frame up on the base, and fix the large wheel in place. Note the little fixing dowels that run through the bottom of the frame and into the frame support.

FIGURE 11-8
Fit the frame on its pegs and test out the movement. If necessary, ease the movement by widening the slot and/or slightly reducing the diameter of the dowels.

3 Fit the frame support to the base slab, set the large wheel on its pivot, and fix the frame in place with dry dowels.

4 Make sure the frame is stable and true—firm, square and free from wobble (Figure 11-7).

5 Set the guide dowels in place in the frame so that they are a tight push fit. Set the rack in place, with its teeth nicely interlocked with the gear wheel, and turn the wheel over to check out the movement. If needs be, adjust the dowels and/or the slot so that the rack is able to move without hindrance (Figure 11-8).

6 Fit the little pall foot in the slot, and fix it in place with a backing plate so that it is loose fitting and able to fall freely (Figure 11-9). Test it out to see if it jams the mechanism.

FIGURE 11-9
The idea is that the pall should be free to rise in its slots, with the little backing plate ensuring that the pall is held square to the front of the frame.

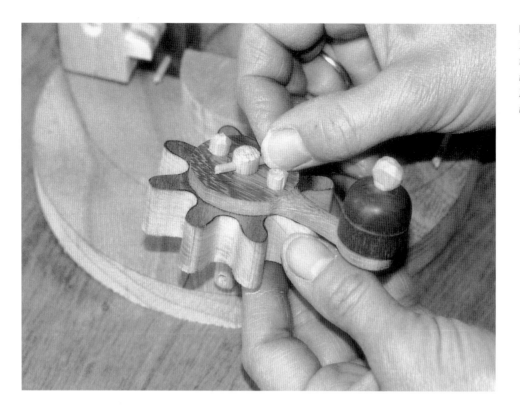

FIGURE 11-10
Have a small wooden pin run-ning through the dowel pivot so that the wheel is free to move. Note the whittled end of the through-knob dowel pin.

FIGURE 11-11
Generally ease the components until the movement is smooth.

FIGURE 11-12
Blind holes are best achieved with a Forstner bit. Note how the pat-tern of decorative holes relates to the pattern of teeth.

FIGURE 11-13
When you are rubbing down, select found items to match the profiles—pencils, plastic pens and the like—and use the finest grade of papers.

7 Set the crank handle on the small wheel, and fit it in place with a couple of dowels so that the crank and the wheel become a single clenched unit (Figure 11-10). Whittle a pivot to run through the knob, so that the end of the pivot becomes a design feature.

8 Set the small wheel in place and fix it at the back with a small wooden pin. Have a trial run and see how the movement functions (Figure 11-11). If one or other of the teeth jams, then ease it with a fold of fine grade sandpaper.

9 When you have achieved a good easy movement—with all the component parts running smoothly one against another—then pencil label the teeth so that you can identically refit.

10 Disassemble the whole works, and spend time adding the decorative features like the pattern of blind holes on the front face of the large wheel (Figure 11-12).

11 Rub all the sawn edges down to a smooth finish. Pay particular attention to the sharp corners of the teeth (Figure 11-13).

12 Finally, give the parts a coat of Danish oil; let it dry. Give the surfaces another swift sanding, glue up, burnish with beeswax polish, and the project is finished.

PROBLEM SOLVING

■ Be mindful that there are three main factors governing the smooth running movement of the teeth: the shape of the teeth, the shape of the gaps between the teeth, and the distance apart of the pivots.

■ If you want to make sure that the movement is going to work the first time around, then it would be a good idea to cut a second frame board made from inexpensive wood. You can thus ensure that the pivot spacings are perfectly placed for the size of your wheels.

■ If you have made a mess-up and you need to alter the position of the pivot holes, then the procedure is as follows: plug and glue the holes with a dowel cut from matching wood, sand back to a smooth finish, and then drill a new hole.

■ Be mindful that a good waxing is one sure-fire way of ensuring that mating components run smooth.

■ Danish oil—meaning a thin varnish.

The Bicycle Chain Machine

PROJECT BACKGROUND

When I was a kid, I used to spend hours taking my bicycle apart. My big thing in life at that time was making bicycles from scrounged parts and then selling them to my schoolmates. I particularly enjoyed taking the drive chain apart.

The bicycle chain is a beautiful item—lots of identical component parts, all made of steel, fitting together to make something both strong and flexible. The earliest known sketches of a bicycle (or drive) chain were made by Leonardo da Vinci. The curious thing about his sketches is that it appears he was inventing components before there was a real need—a bit like inventing the electric coffee maker before the invention of electricity!

PROJECT OVERVIEW

Have a look at the project picture, the working drawings (Figure 12-2A) and the template designs (Figure 12-2B). The machine is made up of a stand, two dowel pivots and two drive-chain wheels, with the actual chain being made up from a large number of identical links. If you look closely at the chain, you will see that the links are first grouped in pairs, with the pairs then being linked to each other. The distance between the centers of neighboring half-circle notches—this being the tooth—is of necessity the same as the distance between the centers of the dowel pins on the drive chain. As the wheels turn, it is the half-circle notches that locate and pull on the chain.

As you might well imagine, the important thing about this project is that the notch centers and the link hole centers be the same. Note how there are 16 notches around the circumference of each wheel, with each notch being centered on the intersection of a radial line and the circumference. See also how the 16 radial lines are equally spaced at 22.5° intervals (360 divided by 16 = 22.5). One look at the various photographs should confirm that this is one of those projects that requires an electric scroll saw.

PROJECT TWELVE: WORKING DRAWING

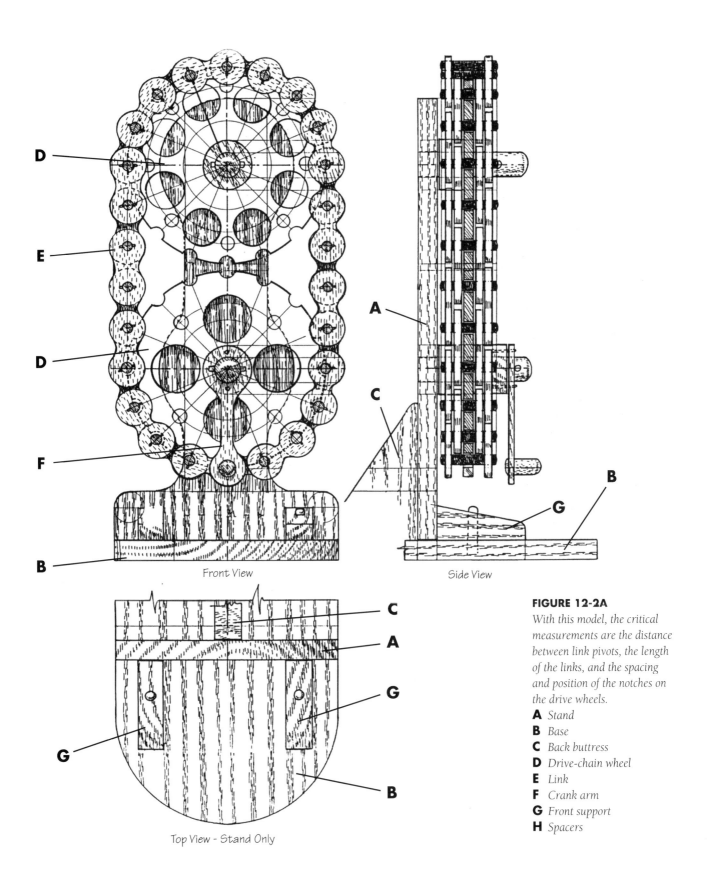

Front View

Side View

Top View - Stand Only

FIGURE 12-2A

*With this model, the critical
measurements are the distance
between link pivots, the length
of the links, and the spacing
and position of the notches on
the drive wheels.*

A *Stand*
B *Base*
C *Back buttress*
D *Drive-chain wheel*
E *Link*
F *Crank arm*
G *Front support*
H *Spacers*

PROJECT TWELVE: TEMPLATE DESIGN

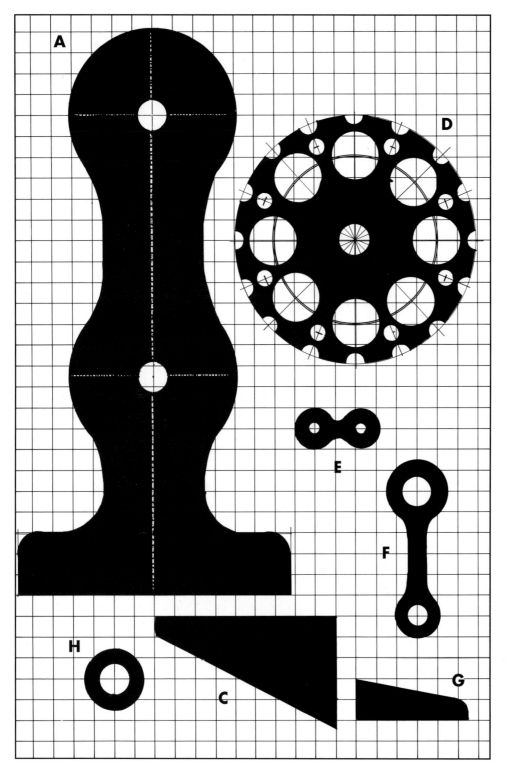

FIGURE 12-2B

The template design at a scale of two grid squares to 1 inch.

A *Stand*
B *Base*
C *Back buttress*
D *Drive-chain wheel*
E *Link*
F *Crank arm*
G *Front support*
H *Spacers*

NOTE

As with any wooden sculpture, the dimensions indicated are starting points only. Modify dimensions, spacers and parts as necessary.

CUTTING LIST

Note: All measurements are in inches, and the sizes allow for generous amounts of waste.

Part	Item	Dimensions T W L
A	Stand	¾ x 7 x 15
B	Base	¾ x 7 x 12
C	Back buttress	¾ x 3 x 5
D	Drive-chain wheel	⅝ x 7 x 7
E	Link	⁵⁄₁₆ x 1½ x 2½
F	Crank arm	⁵⁄₁₆ x 2 x 5
G	Front support	¾ x 1¼ x 3
H	Spacers	1 x 2 x 2

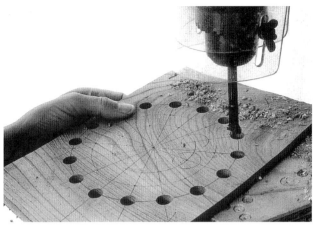

FIGURE 12-3

Having drawn out the 16 radial lines so that they are perfectly placed at 22.5° intervals, then make sure that the drill bit is accurately centered on the radial-circumference intersections.

CHOOSING YOUR WOOD

The two main factors that determine the choice of wood used for the wheels and the chain links, are strength and thickness. While the wheels and the links need to be worked from relatively thin section wood, the wood also needs to be strong. And the wood needs to be easy to work on the scroll saw.

For a mix of these reasons, I decided to use straight-grained pine for the base and the stand, English brown oak for the drive wheels, and pine and cherry for the chain links. I used two wood types for the links because the color contrast made it that much easier to put the chain together.

MAKING THE STAND

1 First study the working drawings (Figure 12-2A) so that you have a clear understanding of the tool and technique implications of the project. Take the wood that you have chosen for the base board, the stand back, the buttress and the two supports, and plane it to a finished thickness of ⅝".

2 Set the stand back board out with a center line that runs in the direction of the grain. Draw in the various lines that go to make up the design. Note that the pivot center points are set 6¼" apart.

3 When you are satisfied with the setting out, then cut the profiles out on the scroll saw.

4 Lastly, decide on the dowel size that you are going to use for the pivots and run them through with the appropriate size bit.

MAKING THE DRIVE-CHAIN WHEELS

1 Having chosen your wood and planed it to a uniform thickness of ³⁄₁₆", set your compass to a radius of 3", and draw out the two 6"-diameter circles.

2 Use the tools of your choice to divide the circle up into 16 identical segments. You can use a protractor or a mix of a compass and the square—there are any number of options. A pretty good way is to set your compass to a guesstimate measurement, and then to repeatedly make step-offs around the circumference, making adjustments until you come up with the correct measurement. Another good way is to cut out a paper circle and then to fold it in half, and half again, and half again, until there are 16 divisions.

3 Draw lines from the 16 step-offs through to the center of the circle, and then take a drill bit of a size to match your dowel and work around the circumference, running holes through the intersections. The important thing here is that the holes are perfectly centered on the circumference-radial intersections, and so placed that all 16 are set the same distance apart from each other (Figure 12-3).

4 Not forgetting that you will at a later stage be drilling a pattern of decorative holes, now is the time to draw in as many guidelines as you think are necessary.

5 Finally, when all the holes are in place, move to the scroll saw and very carefully fret out the circle (Figure 12-4).

MAKING THE LINKS

1 Take the wood that you have chosen for the links and plane it to a finished thickness of about ³⁄₁₆".

2 Cut the wood down so that you have 52 little tablets at about 1⅛"-wide by 2½"-long.

3 Set each tablet out with a center line that runs in the direction of the grain. Take the compass; set it to a radius of about ½". Spike the point on the center line, and, placed as near as it can go to the end of the tablet, draw out the circle. This done, set the compass to the same measurement that you used to work around the circumference of the wheel, and then step-off from the center of the circle to a point on the center line. Draw another 1"-diameter circle at this point. If you have got it right, the distance between centers will be slightly greater than the diameter of the circles. Link the two circles up with a little freehand radius. Repeat this procedure until you have 52 or more links. I decided to make 60—my thinking being that there would be mess-ups along the way.

4 Take a drill bit that matches the diameter of your chosen dowels and run each link through with two holes.

5 With at least 52 links drawn and drilled, then move to the scroll saw and carefully fret them out (Figure 12-5). Don't worry too much if the profiles are askew, as long as the holes are perfectly placed.

6 When you have achieved the 52 links, take a small sharp knife and spend time whittling the sawn edges to a rounded finish. Work with the run of the grain from the peaks down into the dips, and from the peaks and around the ends (Figure 12-6).

PUTTING TOGETHER AND FINISHING

1 When you have achieved all the component parts that go to make up the design, spread them out and generally check them over for fit, finish and number. I say number because it's the easiest thing in the world, with a complex project of this character, to make a mess-up with your counting and finish up with a few links too short. And as no doubt you know, there is nothing quite so annoying in woodwork as getting all ready for the final putting together only to find that you have got to go back to starters and cut more components.

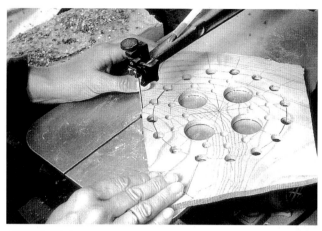

FIGURE 12-4
The line of cut must run very slightly to the waste side of the drawn line. If you fit a new blade and make sure that it is well tensioned, and if you work at an easy pace, then you will finish up with a cut line that requires the minimum of sanding.

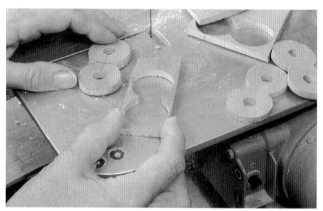

FIGURE 12-5
Bridge the sharp angles between the circles with hand drawn radius curves so that the resultant "8" shape is smooth curved and easy to cut.

FIGURE 12-6
Trim off the sharp corners so that you finish up with form that is round-edged.

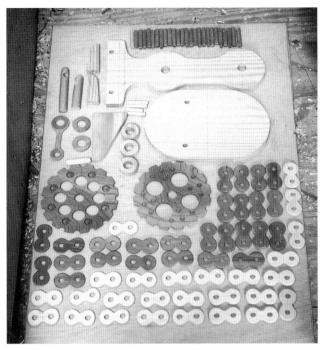

FIGURE 12-7
If, when you line all the component parts up side by side, you see that one or other of the links stands out as being too big, or too small or whatever, then now is the time to throw it out and cut another one.

2 As a trial dry run put together—no fine sanding or glue at this stage—drill, dowel and fit the back board to the base, the buttress to the back of the stand, and the two supports to the front.

3 Set the two main dowel pivots in place in their holes, and slide the various spacers in place (Figure 12-8).

4 Take the links, group them in matched pairs, and set each pair up with dowel pivots (Figure 12-9) so that the links are set together at the middle of the dowel. You need thirteen pairs in all.

5 Set the paired links end to end in a row, and join them together with links set to the outside. You will find that the trick here is in arranging the paired links so that the dowel centers from neighboring groups are nicely matched (Figure 12-10). If necessary, use a fold of sandpaper to make the dowels slightly thinner and/or the holes slightly larger.

6 When you have made the total chain, gently ease the links apart so that the chain fits over the edge of the drive wheels (Figure 12-11).

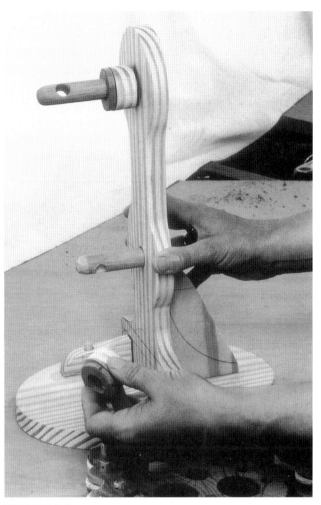

FIGURE 12-8
The buttress and supports ensure that the stand is true and well supported—most important with a machine of this height.

FIGURE 12-9
Fiddle and fuss around until the paired links are well matched, so that the dowels are parallel to each other.

7 At this stage in the operation, you will perhaps find, as you roll the chain over the wheel, that the ends of neighboring links jam. This is because the holes are badly placed and/or the profile has been badly sawn. If this is the case, then take a scrap of sandpaper and gently sand back the shape of the links until the problem is corrected (Figure 12-12).

8 When you have joined up the ends of the chain and generally spaced the links, gently lift the whole works up and set the two wheels on their pivots. If necessary, ease the position of the dowels for best fit (Figure 12-13).

9 Turn the wheels slowly over by hand, and see how the individual links sit one with another. Study the way that the dowel pins come to rest in the notches and how the ends of the links relate to each other. Make adjustments accordingly (Figure 12-14).

10 Fit the spacer and the crank handle, and try everything out for size. Of course, the handle won't actually be turning the wheel at this stage—because it's not pegged to the wheel—but you will at least be able to test out the feel of the machine. The other thing to bear in mind is that you have choices—you can fit the handle to the top pivot, as shown in this photograph, or you can fit it to the bottom, as shown in the working drawings (Figure 12-2A). As to the best position, much depends on the weight of your wood and the size of your hand. For example, if the wood is weighty and the machine top heavy, then it would be a good idea to lower the center of gravity by having the handle on the bottom wheel. But then again, if your hands are large and the turning space is tight, then it might be a better idea to have the handle on the top wheel. It needs thinking about.

11 When you are satisfied with the movement, slowly disassemble the whole works, carefully pencil numbering the links as you go so that you know the order of things.

12 Sand all the components to a fine finish, oil the appropriate surfaces, and then glue up. Finally, burnish all the surfaces with wax, and the project is finished.

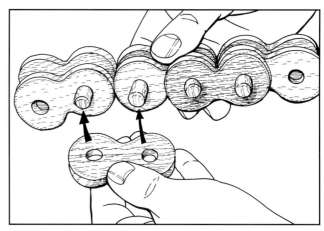

FIGURE 12-10
The outer links need to be matched so that they also hold the dowels parallel to each other.

FIGURE 12-11
Part the links and slide the wheel in place.

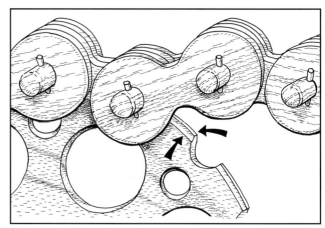

FIGURE 12-12
Once the chain has been fitted, then you can, to a great extent, adjust the fit by sanding a chamfer on the edge of the wheel—on both sides, so that the teeth are slightly beveled.

FIGURE 12-13
The whole thing gets a bit weighty and difficult to handle at this stage, so be on your guard that everything doesn't spring apart. I needed to push a few pegs through some of the dowel pins.

FIGURE 12-14
Make sure that you ease the chain over the wheel so that there is close contact with the link dowels sitting nicely in the wheel notches.

PROBLEM SOLVING

■ The big difficulty with this project is drawing out and cutting the links. The problem isn't that the individual procedures are particularly difficult; only the sum total of cutting each and every link to the same size and drilling perfect-every-time holes calls for a certain regimented way of working. One way out of this problem is to build a drilling jig. In action, you drill one hole, slide the link on the jig, and then drill the other hole. This way of working ensures that the holes are all set the same distance apart.

■ In the light of having made this machine, I think that next time around I will go for much smaller links—say half the size. I will have the wood much thinner, the pivots smaller and the wheels with twice as many notches. I will use a wood like European box or English plum. All

that said, I think that it's vital to have a go at this machine before trying for something smaller.

■ If you find that the movement is loose and sloppy, then it could well be that the links and/or the wheels are badly cut, with the effect that the chain is loose. If this is the case, then you could modify the machine by designing and fitting a mechanism that moved one or other of the wheels up and down and then clamped it in place. You could have the pivot moving in a slot rather than a drilled hole, or you could make the stand so that top and bottom can be moved apart.

■ If you think that the height of the stand is a bit clumsy, then you could change it about so that the two wheels are set side by side—more like a bicycle.

The Wonderful Wilmhurst Machine

PROJECT BACKGROUND

A Wilmhurst machine is an apparatus that is used to demonstrate and produce static electricity. We had such a machine at school. It was a bit like an H.G. Wells time machine—a huge affair with two glass disks, brass rods, metal balls, drive pulleys and crank handles, all mounted on a mahogany base. In action, the massive handle was turned, the two wheels zoomed around in different directions and two metal foil brushes stroked the wheels while they were turning, with the effect that electricity was generated and the thing began to produce a series of snappy, banging and fizzy sparks—really amazing!

PROJECT OVERVIEW

Have a look at the working drawings (Figure 13-2A) and the template designs (Figure 13-2B). The Wilmhurst machine is made up from a base with two stanchions, with all the workings being pivoted on two horizontal dowel shafts. The small pulley wheels on the top shaft are glued to the disk plates, while the large pulley wheels on the bottom shaft are glued to the shaft itself. Perhaps most importantly, one of the two pulley belts (both made of cord or elastic) is twisted into a figure eight so that it reverses the direction of spin of one disk.

PROJECT THIRTEEN: WORKING DRAWING

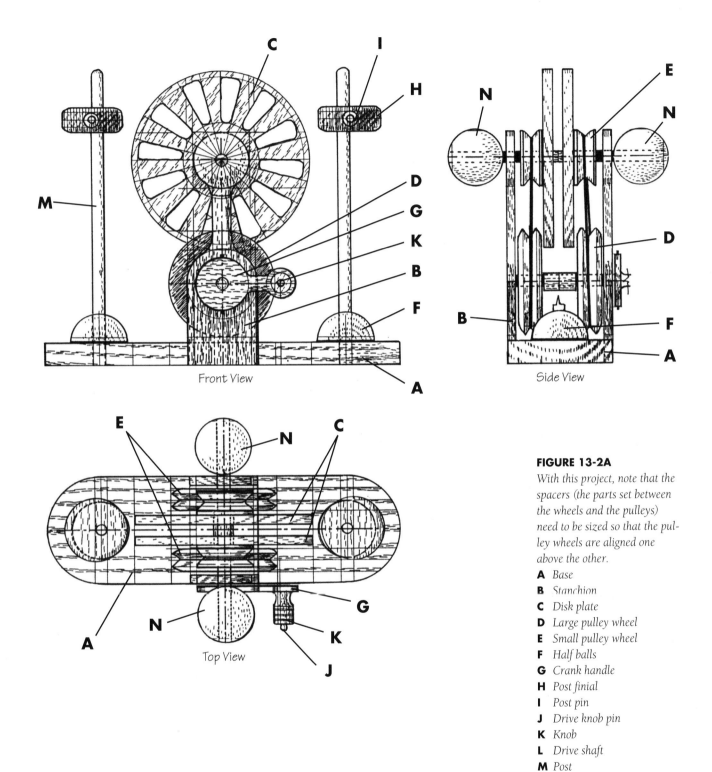

Front View

Side View

Top View

FIGURE 13-2A

With this project, note that the spacers (the parts set between the wheels and the pulleys) need to be sized so that the pulley wheels are aligned one above the other.

A Base
B Stanchion
C Disk plate
D Large pulley wheel
E Small pulley wheel
F Half balls
G Crank handle
H Post finial
I Post pin
J Drive knob pin
K Knob
L Drive shaft
M Post
N Balls

PROJECT THIRTEEN: TEMPLATE DESIGN

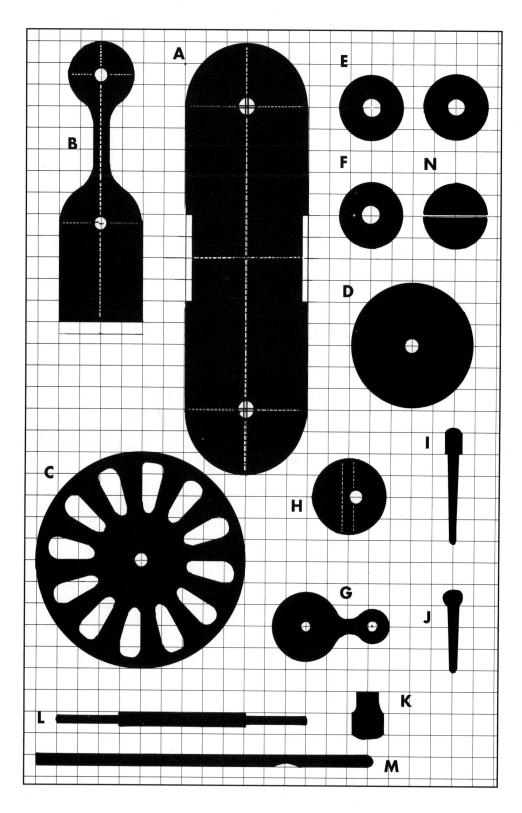

FIGURE 13-2B

The template design at a scale of two grid squares to 1 inch.

A *Base*
B *Stanchion*
C *Disk plate*
D *Large pulley wheel*
E *Small pulley wheel*
F *Half balls*
G *Crank handle*
H *Post finial*
I *Post pin*
J *Drive knob pin*
K *Knob*
L *Drive shaft*
M *Post*
N *Balls*

NOTE

As with any wooden sculpture, the dimensions indicated are starting points only. Modify dimensions, spacers and parts as necessary.

CUTTING LIST

Note: All measurements are in inches, and the sizes allow for a generous amount of waste.

Part	Item	Dimensions T W L
A	Base	¾ x 3½ x 11
B	Stanchion	½ x 2½ x 8
C	Disk plate	½ x 6 x 6
D	Large pulley wheel	¾ x 3½ x 3½
E	Small pulley wheel	¾ x 2½ x 2½
F	Half balls	Cut from 2½" square sections
G	Crank handle	⅜ x 2½ x 3½
H	Post finial	Turned from 2½" square section
I	Post pin	Cut from scrap
J	Drive knob pin	Cut from scrap
K	Knob	Turned from 1" square sections
L	Drive shaft	4" long
M	Post	8½" long
N	Balls	Turned from 2½" square sections

CHOOSING YOUR WOOD

The only real needs for the wood are that the disk plates be made from a wood that can be worked on the scroll saw, and the various balls be worked from a wood that can be turned. We used oak for the disk plates, pine for the stand, beech for the balls and stand supports, an unknown Malaysian wood for the stanchions, a scrap of plum for the two post finials, and offcuts for the rest.

MAKING THE BASE AND STANCHIONS

1 Take the wood for the base slab and plane it to a finished thickness of ⅝".

2 Use the rule, compass and square to set out the profile, and then fret it out on the scroll saw. You should have a base at 3" wide and 10" long, with the ends being based on 3"-diameter half circles.

3 Set the base out with four center lines—one that runs end to end to halve the width, one running across the width to halve the length, and the other two at each end to mark the diameter of the half circle.

4 With all the guidelines in place, use a square to draw the stanchion laps in at ¼" deep and 2" long.

FIGURE 13-3
Run the chisel with a sliding paring action so that the cut goes diagonally across the run of the grain.

FIGURE 13-4
Whittle from the drawn circles, so that the faces of the circles are left in flat relief.

5 Cut the laps with a saw and chisel. First, saw in at each end to establish the depth of the lap, and then use the chisel to make horizontal paring cuts (Figure 13-3). The trick is to make sure that you cut fractionally to the waste side of the drawn lines.

6 Take the wood for the stanchions, plane it to a thickness of ¼", and use a rule and compass to draw out the profile for both stanchions.

7 Fret the profiles out on the scroll saw, so that the bottom 1" is slightly oversize—about 2⅛"—so that the width is too big to fit into the lap.

8 Size the width of the stanchions until they are a tight push fit in the laps.

9 Run the pivot points through with a bit to match the size of your dowel shafts, and use a knife to trim the neck of the stanchion down to a slightly round-edged finish. Work from end to middle so as to avoid running into the end grain curves (Figure 13-4).

MAKING THE DISK PLATES

1 Take your chosen wood and plane it to a finished thickness of about ⁵⁄₁₆". Sight across the wood so as to ensure that it's free from twisting, and then saw it in two so that you have a piece for each circle.

2 Take a piece, set the compass to a radius of 2½", and draw out a single 5"-diameter circle. Now, still working from the same center, draw out circles with radiuses of 1" and 2¼".

3 Use the tools of your choice to divide the circle up into 24 equal 15° segments. I used an engineer's protractor, but you could just as well use a compass by stepping the radius off around the circumference and then quartering the resultant six divisions. You could even do it with a compass and by trial and error.

4 When you have drawn out the circles and their 24 divisions, take a pencil and draw a corner radius in every other division so that you have 12 spokes and 12 round-cornered windows.

5 When you have drawn the circle imagery out on one piece of wood, pin it to the other piece, with the little nails being set in the waste areas well outside the circle.

6 Select a bit size to match the diameter of your chosen dowel, and run a hole through the center of the circle so that it runs through both pieces. Plug the hole with a short length of whittle dowel, then change the drill bit to a smaller size—say about ³⁄₁₆"—and run a hole through every other window.

7 Finally, use the scroll saw to cut out the circle and the windows of waste (Figure 13-5).

MAKING THE PULLEY WHEELS

1 Look at the working drawings (Figure 13-2A); see how you need four pulley wheels in all—two at a 3" diameter, and two at a 1⅝" diameter.

FIGURE 13-5
Note the two holding pegs—one at the center of the circle, the other in the last window to be cut.

FIGURE 13-6
As you work around the wheel, you will need to be constantly changing the angle of cut to suit the run of the grain.

2 Plane your chosen wood down to a ⅝" thickness, draw out the circles, drill the centers out with the appropriate bit size, and then cut the blanks out on the scroll saw.

3 Take the disk blanks one at a time, and first run a pencil center line around the thickness, and then run lines about ⅛" in from the edges.

4 Cut the V-section by first running a stop-cut around the center line. Slice in at an angle into the cut so that the waste falls away, and then deepen the stop-cut, and so on, until the V-section reaches the desired depth. The precise shape of the wheel is a matter of choice—I went for a slightly rounded feel (Figure 13-6), but you could just as well go for a crisp sharp-angled finish.

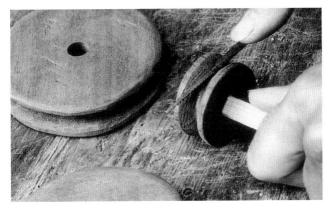

FIGURE 13-7
Though the riffler is a good tool for working hardwood, it's horrible for softwood—be warned.

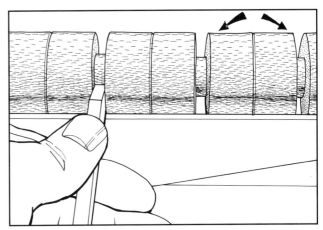

FIGURE 13-8
Sink the waste so that you can shape up the half ball.

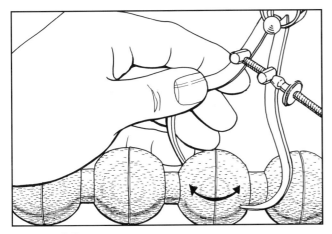

FIGURE 13-9
Make constant checks with the calipers to see how close you are getting to turning a perfect sphere.

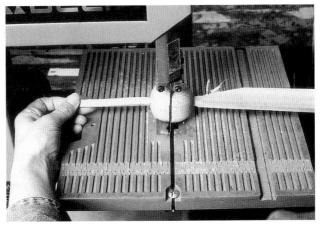

FIGURE 13-10
The sticks ensure that your hands are clear of the blade. DO NOT attempt this procedure without the sticks.

5 When you have whittled the pulleys more or less to shape, bring them to a good finish with a riffler file and the graded sandpapers (Figure 13-7).

MAKING THE BALLS AND POST SUPPORTS

1 Mount your square section wood on the lathe and swiftly turn it down to a smooth cylinder at about 1⅝" diameter.

2 Set the dividers to the diameter of the cylinder, and make step-offs along the cylinder—¼" for tailstock waste, 1⅝" for the first ball, ¼" for parting waste, 1⅝" for the nest ball, and so on along the length of the wood.

3 Take the parting tool and sink the bands of waste in to a depth of about ½" so that you are left with a central core at about ⅝" (Figure 13-8).

4 To make the ball shapes, use the skew chisel to shave the corners off the remaining 1⅝"-diameter sections. If you work backward and forward along the wood with a little-by-little approach, you will eventually finish up with a string of balls—like beads on a necklace (Figure 13-9). Run a little line around each ball to mark the median.

5 Part the balls off from the lathe and select the best of the bunch for the project. You need two complete balls for the end-of-shaft details, and two half balls for the base supports.

6 Run all three balls through with ¼"-diameter holes. Take the ball that needs to be sliced in half, cut a couple of sticks to push in the ball so that you can hold it safely, and then slice it through on the band saw (Figure 13-10).

FIGURE 13-11
Use a sanding board to rub the sawn faces down to a good finish. The stick saves your fingertips from damage.

7 Rub the two half balls down so that the sawn faces sit flat and firm so that the drilled holes are well aligned and square (Figure 13-11).

PUTTING TOGETHER AND FINISHING

1 When you have made all the component parts, gather them on the bench and check them over for problems. Don't worry at this stage about a fine finish because this is a dry run put together, just make sure that the various parts are well cut and sound.

2 Start by setting the two stanchions in place at either side of the base. Trim them to fit and set them upright so that they are at right angles to the base and parallel to each other.

3 Slide the drive shaft through the stanchions—through the bottom hole—and fit the two large pulley wheels and the spacer. Be mindful that the shaft needs to be a loose fit through the stanchions and a tight fit through the wheels (Figure 13-12).

4 Set the disk plate shaft in place, complete with the two disk plates and the small pulley wheels. This time around, the disks and the pulleys need to be a loose fit on the shaft, with the shaft being a loose fit through the stanchions, and the balls being a tight push fit on the ends of the shaft.

5 The order along the length of the shaft is: ball, stanchion, pulley wheel, disk plate, spacer, disk plate, pulley, stanchion and ball.

FIGURE 13-12
Cut the spacer to length so that it pushes the wheels out to within 1⁄16" of the stanchions.

FIGURE 13-13
Measure the spacing and decide if one or more of the parts needs to be modified.

6 Take a rule and decide whether or not one or more of the thicknesses need to be adjusted (Figure 13-13).

7 Consider how the position of the disk plates and the large pulley wheels is to a great extent governed by the spacers between the wheels, and then make adjustments accordingly.

FIGURE 13-14
The ball ends govern the length of the shaft and the consequent placing of the components on the shaft.

FIGURE 13-15
The little peg runs through the side hole and glances off the notched posts to wedge the finial in place.

8 Trim the end of the shaft so as to make a spigot that is a tight fit in the ball (Figure 13-14).

9 The finials at the top of the posts are no more than decorative details but are interesting to make. Held in place by a wedge pin, two holes are drilled through the pill shape so they intersect. The shaft is notched, the pill is slid into position, and a whittled pin is pushed in place so that it locates with the notch (Figure 13-15).

10 The turned knob is held on the crank by means of a whittled pin. The shapes aren't too important as long as the knob is free to turn.

11 At the end of it all, when all the parts are in place, then have a trial run to see if it's going to work. Of course, the plate disks won't turn at this stage, but you will at least be able to see if the large pulley wheels are going to do their stuff.

12 Finally, disassemble the whole works, oil the components, rub down to a good finish, reassemble, wax, fit the drive cords and the machine is ready.

PROBLEM SOLVING

■ If you would like to give the laps a miss and go for another joint, then you could peg the stanchions to the edge of the base. If you go for this option, then you will need to modify the spacers accordingly.

■ While just about everything can be modified—the size of the plates, the height of the stanchions, and all the rest—the only detail that you have to stay with is the alignment of the pulley wheels. The top and bottom wheels must be aligned so that they are set directly one pair above the other.

■ If you don't have a lathe, then you could set the posts directly in the base and miss out the supports, and you could go for pins run through the ends of the drive shaft instead of having the balls.

■ If you have trouble getting the drive cords to grip, then you can use waxed yarn, rubber bands or rubber belts borrowed from children's construction kits, or even the drive belts from video players.

INDEX

A

Assembly, 15, 23-24, 31-32, 52-53, 60, 68-69, 76-77, 83-85, 91-92, 98-100, 106-109, 114-117, 124-125

B

Back boards, 20, 65
Backing disk, 50
Backs, 29, 57, 81, 89
Balls, 123-124
Base boards, 57, 81
Bases, 29, 49, 65, 75, 89, 105, 121-122
Base slab, 12
Belt wheels, 30
Bicycle chain machine, 44, 110-117

C

Camshaft valve, 40, 78-85
Chamber walls, 83, 89
Claw arms, 65
Connecting rod, 14
Control arm, 97-98
Counterbalance guide bridges, 66
Crank disk, 51-52
Crank handle, 31, 106
Crank rods, 97
Cross-coupling union, 74

D

Differential pulley block, 17-25, 34
Disk plates, 122
Drive-chain wheels, 113-114

E

Engine body, 49-50
Excentric squirrel fan, 26-32, 35

F

Fan wheel, 30
Film advancing mechanism, 38, 62-69
Finishing, 15, 23-24, 31-32, 52-53, 60, 68-69, 83-85, 91-92, 98-100, 106-109, 114-117, 124-125
Flywheel, 14
Frames, 29, 105

G

Gallery, 33-45
Gear wheels, 105

H

Holder bars, 22
Holes, drilling, 66
Hook, 21-22

K

Knuckle forks, 73-74

L

Lever & ratchet mechanism, 42, 93-100
Linkage, 90
Links, 114
Lug boards, 89

N

Notched rule, 66

P

Piston block, 12-13
Pistons, 51
Piston washers, 52
Post supports, 123-124
Problem solving, 16, 25, 32, 53, 61, 69, 76-77, 85, 92, 100, 109, 117, 125
Projects
    bicycle chain machine, 44, 110-117
    camshaft valve, 40, 78-85
    differential pulley block, 17-25, 34
    excentric squirrel fan, 26-32, 35
    film advancing mechanism, 38, 62-69
    lever & ratchet mechanism, 42, 93-100
    screw jack, 43, 101-109
    six valve radial engine, 36, 46-53
    steam crank slider mechanism, 9-16, 33
    universal joint, 39, 70-77
    water lift pump, 41, 86-92
    wheel & worm gear mechanism, 37, 54-61
    wonderful Wilmhurst machine, 45, 118-125
Pulley plates, 20
Pulley wheels, 22-23, 66-67, 122-123

R

Ratchet wheel, 20-21
Rack, 105
Rocker arms, 81-82
Rods, 52, 82-83, 90-91

S

Screw jack, 43, 101-109
Side rigger, 20
Six valve radial engine, 36, 46-53
Sliding block, 12-13
Spacers, 51
Stanchions, 12, 74-75, 96-97, 121-122
Stands, 113
Steam crank slider mechanism, 9-16, 33

T

Templates, 11, 19, 28, 48, 56, 64, 72, 80, 88, 95, 103, 104, 112, 120
Toothed wheel, 98

U

Universal joint, 39, 70-77

V

Valve ball, 89
Valve guides, 82-83
Valves, 82

W

Washer handle, 106
Water lift pump, 41, 86-92
Wheels, 57-58
Wheel & worm gear mechanism, 37, 54-61
Wonderful Wilmhurst machine, 45, 118-125
Wood, choosing, 12, 20, 29, 49, 57, 65, 73, 81, 89, 96, 105, 113, 121
Worm, 58-59

More Great Projects for Woodworkers!

Making Wooden Mechanical Models—The original! Discover plans for 15 handsome and incredibly clever machines, with visible wheels, cranks, pistons and other moving parts made of wood. Expertly photographed and complete with materials lists and diagrams, the plans call for a challenging variety of techniques and procedures. #70288/$21.99/144 pages/341 illus./paperback

Beautiful Wooden Gifts You Can Make in a Weekend—This fun and unique book offers you 20 different gift projects that can be built in a couple of days, including step-by-step instructions for jewelry boxes, toys, kitchen accessories, puzzle boxes and more. An easy-to-follow format includes line drawings, photos, illustrations and complete tools and materials lists. #70384/$22.99/128 pages/20 color, 160 b&w illus./paperback

Smart Shelving & Storage Solutions—These innovative and inexpensive storage solutions are perfect for do-it-yourselfers. From book shelves, chests and cabinets to armoires, closet systems and benches, you'll find more than 27 woodworking projects to help you make the most of your space—whether it's under the bed, over the sink or in the garage. #70445/$24.99/144 pages/400 color, b&w illus./paperback

The Weekend Woodworker—A fantastic resource for the straightforward, step-by-step projects you like! This book offers you a range of attractive challenges, from smaller items—such as a stylish CD rack, mailbox or birdhouse—to larger, easy-to-assemble projects, including a wall cupboard, child's bed, computer workstation or coffee table. Each project provides clear and easy step-by-step instructions, photographs and diagrams, ideal for both the beginner and expert. #70456/$22.99/144 pages/200 color photos/paperback

How to Build Classic Garden Furniture—This easy, step-by-step guide will have you anxious to begin crafting this elegant outdoor furniture. The 20 projects are designed to withstand years of outdoor exposure with minimal care, and are versatile enough to compliment any home's style. Each beautiful piece is made easy to accomplish with full-color illustrations, numbered steps, close-up photos and alternatives for design, wood selection and finishing. #70395/$24.99/128 pages/275 color, 69 b&w illus./paperback

Making Elegant Gifts from Wood—Develop your woodworking skills and make over 30 gift-quality projects at the same time? You'll find everything you're looking to create in your gifts—variety, timeless styles, pleasing proportions and imaginative designs that call for the best woods. Plus, technique sidebars and hardware installation tips make your job even easier. #70331/$24.99/ 128 pages/30 color, 120 b&w illus.

Marvelous Wooden Boxes You Can Make—Master woodworker Jeff Greef offers plans for 20 beautiful, functional boxes, complete with drawings, cutting lists, numbered step-by-step instructions and color photographs. #70287/$24.99/144 pages/67 color, 225 b&w illus.

Building Classic Antique Furniture With Pine—This book offers a range of affordable and user-friendly furniture projects, including antique-style tables, desks, cabinets, boxes, chests and more. Each step-by-step project includes numbered steps with photos and drawings, materials lists, a brief description of the function and history of each piece as well as the estimated current market value of both the original piece and the reproduction. #70396/$22.99/ 144 pages/216 color illus./paperback

Display Cabinets You Can Customize—Go beyond building to designing furniture. You'll receive step-by-step instructions to the base projects—the starting points for a wide variety of pieces, such as display cabinets, tables and cases. Then you'll learn about customizing techniques. You'll see how to adapt a glass-front cabinet; put a profile on a cabinet by using molding; get a different look by using stained glass or changing the legs and much more! #70282/$18.99/128 pages/150 b&w illus./paperback

Creating Beautiful Boxes With Inlay Techniques—Now building elegant boxes is easy with this handy reference featuring 13 full-color, step-by-step projects! Thorough directions and precise drawings will have you creating beautiful inlaid boxes with features ranging from handcut dovetails to hidden compartments. #70368/$24.99/128 pages/230 color, 30 b&w illus./paperback

Fast, Easy & Accurate Router Jigs—With the right jigs and fixtures, the router can achieve a range of tasks previously reserved for more cumbersome tools—and with a higher degree of accuracy, efficiency and safety. This ingenious guide features plans for 12 newly perfected router jigs designed to save you time, money and needless frustration. Step-by-step instructions, photos and drawings make it easy to build these projects, which include right angle templates, notching jigs, rounding & tapering jigs, edge guides, lap joint jigs, shop router horse, split pivot fence and more. #70427/$24.99/128 pages/200 b&w illus./paperback

The Woodworker's Visual Guide to Pricing Your Work—With this illustrated pricing guide, you'll be sure to get the best prices for your projects, no matter what your specialty. Each price is determined using proven formulas that factor in labor, materials, overhead and current market value. In addition, you'll receive practical advice about selling and marketing, such as how to run a successful craft show, how to get into juried exhibitions, and how to close a sale. #70443/$21.99/128 pages/200 b&w photos/paperback

Make Your Woodworking Pay for Itself, Revised Edition—Find simple hints for selling your work to generate extra income! You'll find hints on easy ways to save on wood and tools, ideas for projects to sell, guidance for handling money and more! Plus, new information on home-business zoning and tax facts keeps you up-to-date. #70320/$18.99/128 pages/20 b&w illus./paperback

Woodworker's Guide to Pricing Your Work—Turn your hobby into profit! You'll find out how other woodworkers set their prices and sell their products. You'll learn how to estimate average materials cost per project, increase your income with out sacrificing quality or enjoyment, build repeat and referral business, manage a budget and much more! #70268/$18.99/160 pages/paperback

How to Make $40,000 a Year With Your Woodworking—This guide takes the guesswork out of starting and running your own woodworking enterprise. It provides a solid business program using charts, forms and graphs that illustrate how to define objectives, create a realistic plan, market your work, manage your staff and keep good, accurate records with formulas for projecting overhead, labor costs, profit margins, taxes and more. *#70405/$19.99 /128 pages/30 b&w illus./paperback*

Small-Production Woodworking for the Home Shop—Whether fulfilling client orders or making holiday gifts, you'll learn the best ways to "set up shop" in your home for production runs that save time and money. Professional woodworkers share their proven techniques for manufacturing pieces in all shapes, sizes and complexities. *#70385/$23.99/128 pages/180 b&w illus./paperback*

The Woodworker's Guide to Shop Math—A perfect companion to *The Woodworking Handbook*, this hands-on guide takes mathematic principles from the chalkboard to the wood shop, using real-life shop situations to make math easy and practical. Also provided is an overview of basic arithmetic, a review of common units of measurement, and several conversion charts and tables for fractions, multiplication, weights, decimals, volume, area, temperature and more. *#70406/$22.99/208 pages/169 b&w illus./paperback*

Good Wood Handbook, Second Edition—Now in paperback! This handy reference gives you all the information you need to select and use the right wood for the job—before you buy. You'll discover valuable information on a wide selection of commercial softwoods and hardwoods—from common uses, color and grain, to how the wood glues and takes finish. *#70451/$14.99/128 pages/ 250 color illus./paperback*

100 Keys to Woodshop Safety—Make your shop safer than ever with this manual designed to help you avoid potential pitfalls. Tips and illustrations demonstrate the basics of safe shopwork—from using electricity safely and avoiding trouble with hand and power tools to ridding your shop of dangerous debris and handling finishing materials. *#70333/$17.99/64 pages/125 color illus.*